The Alison Burt Cookbook

The Alison Burt
Cookbook

HAMLYN

London · New York · Sydney · Toronto

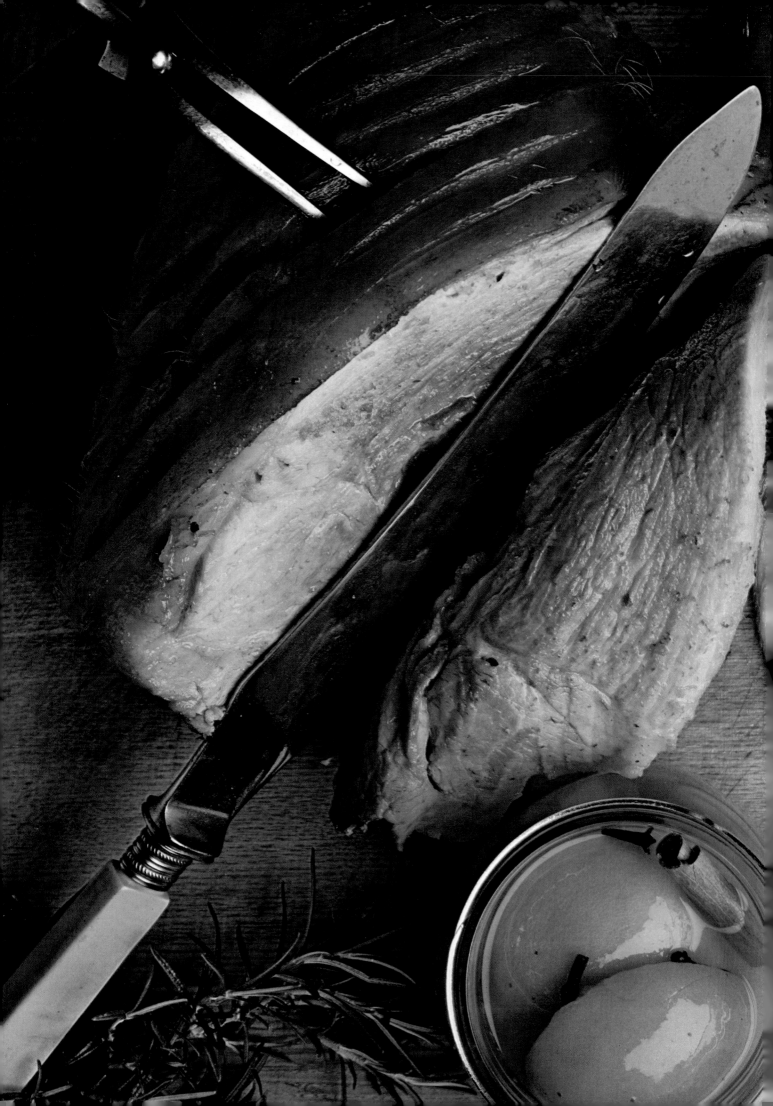

Contents

Photography by Paul Williams
Home economist Carol Bowen

Published by The Hamlyn Publishing Group Limited
London · New York · Sydney · Toronto
Astronaut House, Feltham, Middlesex, England
© Copyright The Hamlyn Publishing Group Limited 1980
ISBN 0 600 30491 4

Printed in Hong Kong

Useful facts and figures

Notes on metrication

In this book quantities are given in metric and Imperial measures. Exact conversion from Imperial to metric measures does not usually give very convenient working quantities and so the metric measures have been rounded off into units of 25 grams. The table below shows the recommended equivalents.

Ounces	Approx g to nearest whole figure	Recommended conversion to nearest unit of 25
1	28	25
2	57	50
3	85	75
4	113	100
5	142	150
6	170	175
7	198	200
8	227	225
9	255	250
10	283	275
11	312	300
12	340	350
13	368	375
14	396	400
15	425	425
16 (1 lb)	454	450
17	482	475
18	510	500
19	539	550
20 (1¼ lb)	567	575

Note: When converting quantities over 20 oz first add the appropriate figures in the centre column, then adjust to the nearest unit of 25. As a general guide, 1 kg (1000 g) equals 2·2 lb or about 2 lb 3 oz. This method of conversion gives good results in nearly all cases, although in certain pastry and cake recipes a more accurate conversion is necessary to produce a balanced recipe.

Liquid measures The millilitre has been used in this book and the following table gives a few examples.

Imperial	Approx ml to nearest whole figure	Recommended ml
¼ pint	142	150 ml
½ pint	283	300 ml
¾ pint	425	450 ml
1 pint	567	600 ml
1½ pints	851	900 ml
1¾ pints	992	1000 ml (1 litre)

Spoon measures All spoon measures given in this book are level unless otherwise stated.

Can sizes At present, cans are marked with the exact (usually to the nearest whole number) metric equivalent of the Imperial weight of the contents, so we have followed this practice when giving can sizes.

Oven temperatures

The table below gives recommended equivalents.

	°C	°F	Gas Mark
Very cool	110	225	¼
	120	250	½
Cool	140	275	1
	150	300	2
Moderate	160	325	3
	180	350	4
Moderately hot	190	375	5
	200	400	6
Hot	220	425	7
	230	450	8
Very hot	240	475	9

Notes for American and Australian users

In America the 8-oz measuring cup is used. In Australia metric measures are now used in conjunction with the standard 250-ml measuring cup. The Imperial pint, used in Britain and Australia, is 20 fl oz, while the American pint is 16 fl oz. It is important to remember that the Australian tablespoon differs from both the British and American tablespoons; the table below gives a comparison. The British standard tablespoon, which has been used throughout this book, holds 17·7 ml, the American 14·2 ml, and the Australian 20 ml. A teaspoon holds approximately 5 ml in all three countries.

British	American	Australia
1 teaspoon	1 teaspoon	1 teaspoon
1 tablespoon	1 tablespoon	1 tablespoon
2 tablespoons	3 tablespoons	2 tablespoons
3½ tablespoons	4 tablespoons	3 tablespoons
4 tablespoons	5 tablespoons	3½ tablespoons

An Imperial/American guide to solid and liquid measures

Solid measures

IMPERIAL	AMERICAN
1 lb butter or margarine	2 cups
1 lb flour	4 cups
1 lb granulated or castor sugar	2 cups
1 lb icing sugar	3 cups
8 oz rice	1 cup

Liquid measures

IMPERIAL	AMERICAN
¼ pint liquid	⅔ cup liquid
½ pint	1¼ cups
¾ pint	2 cups
1 pint	2½ cups
1½ pints	3¾ cups
2 pints	5 cups (2½ pints)

NOTE: When making any of the recipes in this book, only follow one set of measures as they are not interchangeable.

American terms
The list below gives some American equivalents or substitutes for terms and ingredients used in this book.

British	American
cling film	saran wrap
cocktail stick	toothpick
flan tin	pie pan
greaseproof paper	waxed paper
grill	broil
liquidise	blend
mince	grind
packet	package
piping bag	pastry bag
polythene	plastic
roasting tin	roasting pan
sandwich tin	layer cake pan
stoned	pitted
Swiss roll tin	jelly roll pan
top and tail	stem and end

Introduction

This cookery book is a collection of my favourite and most used recipes. During the past few years I have seen both my children and my restaurant grow and have had to rise to the occasion on both fronts. I have also discovered how rewarding it is when a meal is enjoyed–and the diner comes back for more.

The dishes for both family cooking and entertaining are based on popular, well-tried recipes that will be a success every time. Some of these recipes are old favourites, perhaps with a special ingredient that I find makes them especially popular, or maybe the cooking method has been changed to make use of modern cooking techniques and equipment. Other recipes will be new to you: many of these are traditional dishes from other countries or dishes that I have collected, tried and tested over the years and have been approved by family and guests.

Many recipes spring from the interest now being shown in slimming and nutrition. Health food shops and delicatessens are a common sight in shopping centres and the foods they sell open up new horizons in cooking. *Wholewheat flour and other whole grain flours* used in place of white flour give a completely new flavour to your baking and are also higher in nutritional value. Recipes have to be adapted slightly but are basically the same. Bran and wheatgerm, by-products of flour, can also be incorporated into your cooking to make delicious dishes that also improve your diet. *Butter, lard and margarine* are the traditional cooking fats but the advent of the soft 'tub' margarine has changed basic cooking methods with 'one-stage' cookery and all the advantages that this has in saving time. Use a polyunsaturated margarine and again you have the benefit of improving your diet.

Fresh fruit and vegetables are also necessary for a healthy diet (and good cooking) so it is very important to use them whenever possible. Frozen or canned make excellent substitutes but often lack the flavour, appeal and nutritional value of the fresh fruit and vegetables. For the very best cooking, choose dishes according to which fruit and vegetables are in season.

Convenience foods are often taken for granted now. Stock cubes in particular are a well used substitute for the real thing. However, if you do manage to make your own stock, use it instead of a cube. In most recipes the type of stock used is not important and so has not

been specified. Use vegetable, or any meat or poultry stock you have available. The dish will be more individual in its flavour and, of course, cheaper. Cost is important and I would not suggest that you buy essential but expensive ingredients out of season, when frozen or canned are so good. Canned tomatoes and soft fruit are especially useful.

I'm sure that once you try these recipes they will quickly become firm favourites and a reliable addition to your repertoire of dishes to be enjoyed by both family and friends.

Starters and Soups

A meal starter sets the tone for the whole meal and must be chosen with great care. It should complement the main course and whet the appetite, but should not be too filling. It is a good idea to serve small portions but they should taste and look absolutely delicious and be garnished suitably and carefully.

Try to serve a first course that can be prepared well ahead and needs the minimum of last minute attention. Most of the recipes in this chapter fit into this scheme but they vary considerably in their content. Some are suitable for the grandest dinner party but others are very homely; some take time to prepare, others are made of store cupboard and convenience foods, ideal for unexpected guests.

There is a very fine dividing line between starters and main courses. A starter could sometimes be a main course if served in a larger quantity. Soups are particularly tricky to define as they can vary so much. They fall into four main types which are each served in different ways and on different occasions.

★Consommés. These are clear meat soups. To make your own is a bit tedious but the canned variety is very good. Add a little sherry if necessary, or a teaspoon of tomato purée. Serve in small soup cups, garnished with crisp croûtons, diced cooked vegetables, tiny cooked pasta shapes (stars, alphabetti, vermicelli, etc.,) or cooked rice—a quick starter for the grandest dinner party.

★Thick and cream soups. These are made from ingredients that are in season. An electric blender is useful to purée cooked vegetables for a really smooth, delicious and economical soup. Serve in soup cups garnished with crisp croûtons or an appropriate vegetable garnish. Good enough for any occasion—perhaps add a swirl of cream for a really special dinner.

★Broths and chowders. These are not really meal starters but constitute a meal in themselves. Broths are frequently served as both the soup and main course, the meat and vegetables that are cooked in the soup are removed so that the liquid is drunk first, followed by the meat. Serve for easy and nourishing family meals, piping hot on a deep but wide plate—lovely with homemade or French bread.

★Cold soups are the hostess's answer to hot summer evenings. Made well ahead and chilled in the refrigerator until needed, they make a suitable and refreshing start to any dinner. Serve in chilled soup cups, garnished with crisp croûtons, a suitable vegetable or a sprig of a fresh herb—parsley, mint, chervil, as available.

Convenience foods tend to reign supreme in the soup world. Soups and stock cubes are so easy to store and are ready for immediate use. They are short cuts that are permissible if you are really pressed for time, but nothing can rival homemade dishes prepared using fresh ingredients.

Avocado Cocktail

SERVES 4

METRIC/IMPERIAL	AMERICAN
350 g/12 oz small peeled shrimps or prawns	¾ lb small shelled shrimp
2 hard-boiled eggs	2 hard-cooked eggs
shredded lettuce	shredded lettuce
lemon slices for garnish	lemon slices for garnish
Avocado sauce:	*Avocado sauce:*
1 very ripe avocado	1 very ripe avocado
1 tablespoon lemon juice	1 tablespoon lemon juice
2 tablespoons soured cream	3 tablespoons dairy sour cream
2 spring onions, finely chopped	2 scallions, finely chopped
6 stuffed green olives, finely chopped	6 stuffed green olives, finely chopped
2 tablespoons mayonnaise	3 tablespoons mayonnaise
salt and pepper	salt and pepper

Chill the shrimps and reserve 8 for garnishing. Separate the egg yolks and whites, sieve the yolks and chop the whites finely.

Make the sauce. Peel the avocado, remove the stone and mash well, gradually adding the lemon juice. Stir in all the remaining ingredients. Taste and adjust seasoning.

Put some lettuce in the base of 4 tall glasses. Arrange some shrimps on top and sprinkle with the egg white and yolk. Cover with sauce. Repeat the layers once more.

Chill slightly and serve garnished with lemon slices and the reserved shrimps.

Cream Cheese and Cucumber Mousse

SERVES 6

METRIC/IMPERIAL	AMERICAN
1 cucumber	1 large cucumber
salt and pepper	salt and pepper
225 g/8 oz cream cheese	1 cup cream cheese
1 tablespoon grated onion	1 tablespoon grated onion
1 (14-g/½-oz) envelope powdered gelatine	2 (7-g/¼-oz) envelopes gelatin
5 tablespoons warm water	6 tablespoons warm water
2 tablespoons white wine	3 tablespoons white wine
1 teaspoon castor sugar	1 teaspoon sugar
1 teaspoon curry powder	1 teaspoon curry powder
150 ml/¼ pint whipping cream	⅔ cup whipping cream
For garnish:	*For garnish:*
slices of cucumber	slices of cucumber
sprigs of watercress	sprigs of watercress

Peel the cucumber and grate it coarsely. Put it in a colander and sprinkle liberally with salt. Put aside for 30 minutes for excess liquid to drain off.

Mix the cream cheese and onion together well. Dissolve the gelatine in the water then add the wine, sugar and curry powder and allow to cool without setting.

Beat the gelatine into the cream cheese and mix in the well-drained cucumber. Whip the cream and fold in. Taste and adjust seasoning.

Put into individual serving pots (large ramekins are ideal) and chill. Serve garnished with cucumber and watercress.

Salmon and Cucumber Rolls

Smoked salmon is lovely but rather expensive: stretch it to serve more people with this recipe for an ideal dinner party starter.

SERVES 8

METRIC/IMPERIAL	AMERICAN
1 recipe Cream Cheese and Cucumber Mousse	1 recipe Cream Cheese and Cucumber Mousse
8 very thin slices smoked salmon	8 very thin slices smoked salmon
For garnish:	*For garnish:*
wedges of lemon	wedges of lemon
sprigs of watercress	sprigs of watercress

Make the Cream Cheese and Cucumber Mousse and allow it to set in one bowl.

Spread the smoked salmon on the work surface and divide the mousse equally between the slices. Roll up and place on a serving plate. Chill.

Garnish with the wedges of lemon and watercress and serve with very thin brown bread and butter.

Herbed Cheese Soufflé

SERVES 4–6

METRIC/IMPERIAL	AMERICAN
150 ml/¼ pint milk	⅔ cup milk
1 bouquet garni	1 bouquet garni
25 g/1 oz butter	2 tablespoons butter
25 g/1 oz plain flour	¼ cup all-purpose flour
salt and pepper	salt and pepper
pinch of dry mustard	dash of dry mustard
4 egg yolks	4 egg yolks
100 g/4 oz Cheddar cheese, grated	1 cup grated Cheddar cheese
1 tablespoon chopped parsley	1 tablespoon chopped parsley
5 egg whites	5 egg whites

Put the milk and bouquet garni into a saucepan. Bring to the boil then cover the pan and leave until cold again. Strain the milk.

Melt the butter, stir in the flour and cook, stirring, for 1 – 2 minutes. Stir in the flavoured milk and bring to the boil, stirring all the time. Boil for 2 minutes and add the seasoning and mustard. Remove the pan from the heat and beat in the egg yolks one at a time. Stir in the cheese and parsley.

Whisk the egg white until it stands in soft peaks. Fold the egg white into the cheese mixture using a metal spoon.

Spoon the soufflé mixture into a greased 15-cm/6-inch soufflé dish. Cook in a moderately hot oven (190°C, 375°F, Gas Mark 5) for 30 – 40 minutes, or until well risen, firm and golden.

Serve straightaway – a soufflé does not like to be kept waiting.

Tuna Sunflower Pâté

SERVES 4

Toasted sunflower seeds are available from health food shops.

METRIC/IMPERIAL	AMERICAN
1 (198-g/7-oz) can tuna	1 (7-oz) can tuna
1 tablespoon brandy	1 tablespoon brandy
1 hard-boiled egg, chopped	1 hard-cooked egg, chopped
100 g/4 oz cream cheese	$\frac{1}{4}$ lb cream cheese
2 tablespoons toasted sunflower seeds	3 tablespoons toasted sunflower seeds
salt and pepper	salt and pepper
hot toast for serving	hot toast for serving

Put the tuna (including the oil) into an electric blender, add the brandy and blend until smooth. Blend in the hard-boiled egg.

Put into a bowl and beat in the cream cheese and sunflower seeds. Taste and season.

Put the pâté into a bowl and chill until firm.

Serve with hot, freshly cooked toast.

Brussels Chicken Pâté

SERVES 8–10

METRIC/IMPERIAL	AMERICAN
10–12 rashers streaky bacon	10–12 bacon slices
1.5 kg/3 lb chicken	3 lb chicken
liver from chicken	liver from chicken
450 g/1 lb belly pork	1 lb salt pork
pinch of ground allspice	dash of ground allspice
pinch of ground cloves	dash of ground cloves
$\frac{1}{2}$ teaspoon dried thyme	$\frac{1}{2}$ teaspoon dried thyme
1 clove garlic, crushed	1 clove garlic, crushed
salt and pepper	salt and pepper
3 tablespoons brandy	$\frac{1}{4}$ cup brandy
1 egg	1 egg
2 bay leaves	2 bay leaves
wholemeal toast for serving	whole meal toast for serving

Remove the rinds from the bacon and line a 1-kg/2-lb loaf tin with the rashers.

Remove all the chicken meat from the bones. Slice the breast meat as thinly as possible. Mince the remaining chicken once, then again with the liver and pork.

Mix the meat with the allspice, cloves, thyme, garlic, seasoning, brandy and egg. Press half the mixture into the lined tin, cover with the sliced meat and then with the remaining mixture. Put the bay leaves on top and cover with any remaining rashers.

Put the pâté in a water bath with 2·5 cm/1 inch water. Bake in a cool oven (150°C, 300°F, Gas Mark 2) for 2 hours or until firm and cooked.

Cool the pâté then cover with paper and put a heavy weight on top to press it. Leave overnight.

Serve sliced, with warm wholemeal toast.

Asparagus and Ham Pancakes

SERVES 6

METRIC/IMPERIAL	AMERICAN
Pancakes:	*Pancakes:*
100 g/4 oz plain flour	1 cup all-purpose flour
pinch of salt	dash of salt
1 egg	1 egg
1 egg yolk	1 egg yolk
300 ml/½ pint water	1¼ cups water
lard for frying	shortening for frying
Filling:	*Filling:*
65 g/2½ oz butter	5 tablespoons butter
65 g/2½ oz plain flour	scant ⅔ cup all-purpose flour
300 ml/½ pint milk	1¼ cups milk
1 chicken stock cube	1 chicken bouillon cube
225 g/8 oz ham	½ lb cooked ham
100 g/4 oz Cheddar cheese, grated	1 cup grated Cheddar cheese
salt and pepper	salt and pepper
1 (283-g/10-oz) can asparagus	1 (10-oz) can asparagus

Sift the flour and salt into a bowl. Make a well in the centre and put in the egg and egg yolk. Using a wire whisk, beat the mixture, gradually mixing in the water to make a thin batter.

Lightly grease a small 15-cm/6-inch frying pan with lard and heat until the lard begins to smoke a little. Add 2 tablespoons of the batter and tilt the pan so that it is just evenly covered with batter. Cook until lightly browned underneath then flip the pancake over and cook the underside until browned. Put on a plate to cool. Cook the other pancakes in the same way and stack them one on top of the other.

To make the filling, put the butter, flour, milk and stock cube into a saucepan and bring to the boil, whisking all the time with a balloon whisk. Boil gently for 2 minutes. Chop the ham and stir into the sauce with the cheese. Season to taste.

Spread the sauce equally on the pancakes. Drain the asparagus and divide equally between the pancakes. Roll up the pancakes and put close together in an ovenproof dish. Cook in a moderately hot oven (190°C, 375°F, Gas Mark 5) for 15–20 minutes or until thoroughly reheated. Serve immediately.

Monterey Devilled Seafood

SERVES 4–6

METRIC/IMPERIAL	AMERICAN
450 g/1 lb cooked shellfish (mussels, cockles, prawns, crab meat, lobster, scallops, as available)	1 lb cooked shellfish (mussels, cockles, shrimp, crab meat, lobster, scallops, as available)
225 g/8 oz white fish fillet	½ lb white fish fillet
1 tablespoon lemon juice	1 tablespoon lemon juice
25 g/1 oz butter	2 tablespoons butter
25 g/1 oz plain flour	¼ cup all-purpose flour
300 ml/½ pint milk	1¼ cups milk
1 teaspoon Worcestershire sauce	1 teaspoon Worcestershire sauce
1 tablespoon dry mustard	1 tablespoon dry mustard
salt and pepper	salt and pepper
25 g/1 oz fresh breadcrumbs	½ cup fresh soft bread crumbs
25 g/1 oz butter, melted	2 tablespoons butter, melted
For garnish:	*For garnish:*
slices of lemon	slices of lemon
chopped parsley	chopped parsley

Prepare the shellfish. Discard any mussels and cockles which do not close when tapped, then cook in 1 cm/½ inch boiling water. Cover the pan and shake over a high heat until they open. Discard any which do not open. Remove the fish from the shells. Poach scallops in milk for 7–10 minutes. Poach the fish fillet in enough water to cover for 15–20 minutes. Drain and flake the flesh.

Cut all the seafood into bite-sized pieces and sprinkle with the lemon juice.

Put the butter, flour and milk into a saucepan and bring to the boil, whisking all the time with a balloon whisk. Boil for 1–2 minutes, stirring continuously. Whisk in the Worcestershire sauce and mustard. Stir in the seafood and fish. Taste and season.

Divide between four or six individual dishes, sprinkle with breadcrumbs and drizzle the melted butter over the top.

Cook in a moderately hot oven (200°C, 400°F, Gas Mark 6) for 20 minutes, or until browned on top and heated through. Garnish with slices of lemon and chopped parsley.

Lemon Soup

SERVES 4

An unusual and very elegant starter for a dinner party.

METRIC/IMPERIAL	AMERICAN
40 g/1½ oz butter	3 tablespoons butter
1 onion, finely chopped	1 onion, finely chopped
25 g/1 oz plain flour	¼ cup all-purpose flour
600 ml/1 pint chicken stock	2½ cups chicken stock
finely grated rind and juice of 1 lemon	finely grated rind and juice of 1 lemon
4 tablespoons cream	⅓ cup cream
slices of lemon to garnish	slices of lemon to garnish

Heat the butter in a saucepan and fry the onion until softened but not browned. Add the flour and cook, stirring, for 2–3 minutes.

Mix in the stock with the lemon rind and juice. Bring to the boil, stirring all the time. Cover the pan and simmer for 20 minutes.

Serve the soup in four individual soup bowls. Swirl a tablespoon of cream in each and float a slice of lemon on top just before serving.

Mushroom and Garlic Soup

SERVES 6

METRIC/IMPERIAL	AMERICAN
225 g/8 oz mushrooms	½ lb mushrooms
1 onion	1 onion
2 cloves garlic, crushed	2 cloves garlic, crushed
75 g/3 oz butter	6 tablespoons butter
50 g/2 oz plain flour	½ cup all-purpose flour
900 ml/1½ pints stock	3¾ cups stock
1 bay leaf	1 bay leaf
salt and pepper	salt and pepper
2 tablespoons soy sauce	3 tablespoons soy sauce
1 (142-ml/5-fl oz) carton soured cream	1 (5-fl oz) carton dairy sour cream
1 tablespoon chopped parsley	1 tablespoon chopped parsley

Chop the mushrooms and onion finely and mix with the garlic. Melt the butter in a saucepan and fry the vegetables until softened.

Stir in the flour and cook, stirring all the time, for 2–3 minutes. Mix in the stock and bring to the boil, still stirring continuously.

Add the bay leaf and seasoning then cover and cook gently for 15 minutes.

Stir the soy sauce into the soured cream and whisk into the soup. Reheat but do not boil. Taste and adjust the seasoning then remove the bay leaf. Stir in the parsley and serve as soon as possible.

Cream of Shellfish Soup

SERVES 6–8

A luxurious soup for entertaining. Make fish stock by cooking a fish head and any skin and bones with a sliced onion, carrot and seasoning, in water for 30 minutes. Strain before use.

METRIC/IMPERIAL	AMERICAN
600 ml/1 pint cockles or mussels	2½ cups cockles or mussels
6 tablespoons white wine	½ cup white wine
1 bay leaf	1 bay leaf
3–4 peppercorns	3–4 peppercorns
1 litre/1¾ pints fish stock	4¼ cups fish stock
40 g/1½ oz butter	3 tablespoons butter
40 g/1½ oz plain flour	6 tablespoons all-purpose flour
225 g/8 oz peeled prawns	½ lb shelled shrimp
100 g/4 oz crab or lobster meat, flaked	¼ lb crab or lobster meat, flaked
salt and pepper	salt and pepper
150 ml/¼ pt double cream	⅔ cup heavy cream
2 egg yolks	2 egg yolks

Discard any cockles or mussels which do not close when tapped. Put the shellfish in a saucepan with the wine, bay leaf and peppercorns. Cook over a high heat, shaking the pan occasionally. After 5 minutes all the shellfish will have opened. Any that have not should be discarded. Strain the liquid reserving both the liquid and the shellfish; mussels can be left in the shells if liked.

Put the stock in a saucepan with the butter and flour. Bring to the boil, whisking all the time with a balloon whisk. Boil for 1–2 minutes. Add the prawns and crab or lobster with the strained cooking liquid. Combine the cream and egg yolks and add to the soup. Reheat without boiling. Season to taste.

Spicy Tomato Soup

SERVES 4

METRIC/IMPERIAL	AMERICAN
450 g/1 lb red ripe tomatoes or 1 (396-g/14-oz) can tomatoes	1 lb red ripe tomatoes or 1 (14-oz) can tomatoes
25 g/1 oz butter	2 tablespoons butter
1 onion, chopped	1 onion, chopped
1 tablespoon plain flour	1 tablespoon all-purpose flour
½ teaspoon paprika	½ teaspoon paprika pepper
2 teaspoons tomato purée	2 teaspoons tomato paste
900 ml/1½ pints stock	3¾ cups stock
1 bouquet garni	1 bouquet garni
pinch of ground nutmeg	dash of ground nutmeg
pinch of ground cloves	dash of ground cloves
salt and pepper	salt and pepper
1 tablespoon long-grain rice	1 tablespoon long-grain rice
2 tablespoons sherry (optional)	3 tablespoons sherry (optional)

Chop the tomatoes coarsely. Melt the butter in a large saucepan and fry the onion until softened. Stir in the flour and paprika then the tomato purée, stock, bouquet garni, nutmeg, cloves and seasoning. Bring to the boil, stirring all the time, then simmer for 30 minutes.

Strain the soup through a sieve, pressing with a wooden spoon to get as much through as possible.

Return the soup to the rinsed pan. Add the rice and sherry, bring to the boil and cook for 20 minutes. Taste and adjust the seasoning. Serve piping hot.

Chilled Summer Soup

SERVES 6

METRIC/IMPERIAL	AMERICAN
4 red ripe tomatoes, peeled and coarsely chopped	4 red ripe tomatoes, peeled and coarsely chopped
3 tablespoons diced cucumber	$\frac{1}{4}$ cup diced cucumber
3 tablespoons diced green pepper	$\frac{1}{4}$ cup diced green pepper
3 tablespoons finely sliced celery	$\frac{1}{4}$ cup finely sliced celery
$\frac{1}{2}$ small onion, grated	$\frac{1}{2}$ small onion, grated
300 ml/$\frac{1}{2}$ pint tomato juice	$1\frac{1}{4}$ cups tomato juice
1 (298-g/10$\frac{1}{2}$-oz) can condensed consommé, diluted	1 (10$\frac{1}{2}$-oz) can condensed consommé, diluted
1 tablespoon wine vinegar	1 tablespoon wine vinegar
1 clove garlic, crushed	1 clove garlic, crushed
salt and pepper	salt and pepper
1 tablespoon chopped parsley	1 tablespoon chopped parsley
2 (142-ml/5-fl oz) cartons soured cream for serving	2 (5-fl oz) cartons dairy sour cream for serving

Put all the ingredients except the soured cream in a large bowl and stir well. Cover and chill for at least 3 – 4 hours.

Serve in chilled bowls with a spoonful of soured cream to garnish.

Thick Onion Soup

SERVES 4–6

METRIC/IMPERIAL	AMERICAN
50 g/2 oz butter	$\frac{1}{4}$ cup butter
450 g/1 lb onions, thinly sliced	1 lb onions, thinly sliced
2 rashers streaky bacon, chopped	2 bacon slices, chopped
2 sticks celery, chopped	2 stalks celery, chopped
900 ml/1$\frac{1}{2}$ pints stock	3$\frac{3}{4}$ cups stock
1 bouquet garni	1 bouquet garni
2 tablespoons cornflour	3 tablespoons cornstarch
300 ml/$\frac{1}{2}$ pint milk	1$\frac{1}{4}$ cups milk
salt and pepper	salt and pepper

Heat the butter in a large saucepan and fry the onion, bacon and celery until softened but not browned, about 10–15 minutes. Add the stock and bouquet garni and bring to the boil. Cover and simmer for about 30 minutes, or until the onion is very tender.

Reserve some of the onion rings for garnish. Remove the bouquet garni. Blend the soup until smooth in an electric blender.

Return the soup to the rinsed pan. Mix the cornflour with the milk and stir into the pan. Bring to the boil, stirring all the time. Simmer for 2 minutes. Taste and adjust the seasoning. Return the reserved onion rings to the soup. Serve piping hot.

For a family supper, heat some sliced frankfurters in the soup and serve it with crusty wholemeal bread.

Tuna Rice Chowder

SERVES 4–6

METRIC/IMPERIAL
1 small onion, thinly sliced
100 g/4 oz long-grain rice
1 (227-g/8-oz) can
   tomatoes
1 litre/1¾ pints stock
1 bay leaf
1 (198-g/7-oz) can tuna
15 g/½ oz margarine or
   butter
15 g/½ oz plain flour
300 ml/½ pint milk
salt and pepper
1 tablespoon chopped
   parsley

AMERICAN
1 small onion, thinly sliced
generous ½ cup long-grain
   rice
1 (8-oz) can tomatoes
4¼ cups stock
1 bay leaf
1 (7-oz) can tuna
1 tablespoon margarine or
   butter
2 tablespoons all-purpose
   flour
1¼ cups milk
salt and pepper
1 tablespoon chopped
   parsley

Put the onion, rice, tomatoes, stock and bay leaf into a saucepan. Bring to the boil, cover and simmer for 20 minutes.

Drain the tuna, flake with a fork and stir into the saucepan.

Meanwhile put the margarine or butter, flour and milk into another saucepan. Bring to the boil whisking continuously with a balloon whisk. Boil for 2 minutes then season to taste. Stir the sauce into the soup with the parsley. Taste and adjust the seasoning then serve as soon as possible.

Tomato Gumbo

SERVES 4

METRIC/IMPERIAL
1 tablespoon olive oil
50 g/2 oz ham, chopped
1 potato, diced
1 onion, chopped
300 ml/½ pint stock
1 (396-g/14-oz) can
   tomatoes
salt and pepper
pinch of ground mixed
   spice
1 teaspoon cornflour
2 tablespoons milk
1 canned pimiento, chopped
   (optional)
1 tablespoon chopped
   chives

AMERICAN
1 tablespoon olive oil
¼ cup chopped cooked ham
1 potato, diced
1 onion, chopped
1¼ cups stock
1 (14-oz) can tomatoes
salt and pepper
dash of ground mixed spice
1 teaspoon cornstarch
3 tablespoons milk
1 canned pimiento,
   chopped (optional)
1 tablespoon chopped
   chives

Heat the oil in a saucepan and fry the ham, potato and onion until the onion is softened. Add the stock, tomatoes, seasoning and spice. Bring to the boil, cover and simmer for 20 minutes.

Mix the cornflour with the milk and stir into the soup. Simmer for 1–2 minutes. Stir in the pimiento. Taste, adjust the seasoning and serve very hot, sprinkled with chives.

Quick Oxtail Soup with Lentils

SERVES 4

Other varieties of soups could be used instead of oxtail to make this very substantial soup. Serve with wholemeal bread.

METRIC/IMPERIAL	AMERICAN
1 (298-g/10½-oz) can condensed oxtail soup	1 (10½-oz) can condensed oxtail soup
600 ml/1 pint stock	2½ cups stock
3 tablespoons lentils	¼ cup lentils
2 sticks celery, chopped	2 stalks celery, chopped
1 onion, finely chopped	1 onion, finely chopped
2 tomatoes, peeled and chopped	2 tomatoes, peeled and chopped
salt and pepper	salt and pepper

Put all the ingredients in a saucepan. Bring to the boil, cover and simmer for 30 minutes.

Serve piping hot.

Country Vegetable Broth

SERVES 4

Ask your butcher for some ham bones or, if he cooks his own hams, he might be able to give you ham stock; check that it's not too salty.

METRIC/IMPERIAL	AMERICAN
175 g/6 oz split peas	¾ cup split peas
900 ml/1½ pints water	3¾ cups water
450 g/1 ib ham bones	1 lb ham bones
225 g/8 oz carrots, sliced	½ lb carrots, sliced
1 onion, finely chopped	1 onion, finely chopped
100 g/4 oz ham, diced	½ cup diced cooked ham
1 tablespoon chopped parsley or mint	1 tablespoon chopped parsley or mint
salt and pepper	salt and pepper
1 teaspoon prepared mild mustard	1 teaspoon prepared mild mustard

Put the peas, water and ham bones in a large saucepan. Bring to the boil, cover and simmer for 1 hour.

Remove the bones, scrape off and chop the meat. Return the meat to the soup and add the carrots, onion and ham. Simmer for a further 30–45 minutes.

Stir in the parsley or mint. Season carefully – it may not need any salt. Add the mustard.

Serve piping hot.

Belgian Fish Broth

SERVES 4–6

This is almost a complete meal in itself. Serve it with crusty bread for a special but informal lunch or supper.

METRIC/IMPERIAL	AMERICAN
900 g/2 lb white fish fillet, skinned	2 lb white fish fillet, skinned
50 g/2 oz butter	¼ cup butter
2 carrots, thinly sliced	2 carrots, thinly sliced
2 leeks, thinly sliced	2 leeks, thinly sliced
4 sticks celery, thinly sliced	4 stalks celery, thinly sliced
25 g/1 oz plain flour	¼ cup all-purpose flour
300 ml/½ pint water	1¼ cups water
150 ml/¼ pint whipping cream	⅔ cup whipping cream
salt and pepper	salt and pepper

Cut the fish into bite-sized pieces. Heat the butter in a large saucepan and fry the carrot, leek and celery very gently for 10 minutes, stirring occasionally. Sprinkle in the flour and cook, stirring, for 1 – 2 minutes. Gradually mix in the water then bring to the boil. Add the fish. Cover the pan and simmer for 15 minutes. Stir in the cream, reheat without boiling. Taste and adjust the seasoning.

Serve as soon as possible in hot serving bowls.

Family Meals

Cooking for a family every day and knowing their likes and dislikes is part of being a housewife. You cook dishes which fit in with everyone's plans and provide a good balanced diet. It is easier if you mentally plan the week ahead and then write a shopping list so that you have everything to hand when you need it. You can also budget, as most people have to keep within a certain sum of money. Entertaining is different and can be more lavish, but when cooking for the family, economy is usually very important.

Every family is different, a fact brought home to me when my children bring home unexpected guests to supper. I am serving what I *know* everyone loves, but this child says "I don't like this." Then is the time to quickly fry up a hamburger or fish finger from the freezer. For their speed in cooking, these foods are useful, but they should really only be used as stopgaps. Children very quickly get used to eating soft, easy-to-chew foods which have a bland taste. Educate them on to more interesting "proper" food before it becomes a habit.

For working mothers, when time to shop and cook is at a premium, a freezer is very useful. I have never met anyone yet who says it saves money, but it certainly saves time. Cook casseroles and do your baking when it is convenient. Keep the freezer stocked with meat, fish, bread and some fruit and vegetables – it cuts out those last minute shopping trips.

The quality of food is a very important factor in good cooking. Choose your shops carefully then shop at the same greengrocers, butchers and fishmongers all the time, whether you are buying small quantities or in bulk. This way you get to know the experts who will advise you as to the correct cuts of meat to use, whether or not vegetables and fruit are good value and when the different varieties of fish are at their peak in quality. You will also be able to complain more easily, if necessary!

The recipes in this chapter are economical, and mostly quick to prepare. They fit many different occasions of family life and my family, at least, enjoys eating them – I hope yours does too.

Boiled Salt Beef or Ham

SERVES 6 – 8

Salt beef and ham are very similar. They are both very suitable for this recipe – only the cooking times are different. For economy choose silverside or topside of beef or collar or forehock of ham.

METRIC/IMPERIAL	AMERICAN
1·5 kg/3 lb joint salt beef or ham	3 lb joint corned beef brisket
2 onions, quartered	2 onions, quartered
1 large carrot, thinly sliced	1 large carrot, thinly sliced
8 cloves	8 cloves
8 peppercorns	8 peppercorns
1 bay leaf	1 bay leaf
25 g/1 oz brown sugar	2 tablespoons brown sugar
1 stock cube	1 bouillon cube
Dumplings:	*Dumplings:*
100 g/4 oz plain wholemeal flour	1 cup whole meal flour
1 teaspoon baking powder	1 teaspoon baking powder
pinch of salt	dash of salt
50 g/2 oz shredded suet	6 tablespoons chopped suet
½ teaspoon dried mixed herbs	½ teaspoon dried mixed herbs
cold water to mix	cold water to mix

Put the beef or ham in a large saucepan. Add the onion, carrot, cloves, peppercorns, bay leaf, sugar, stock cube and enough cold water to just cover. Bring to the boil, cover the pan and simmer according to the following times. For beef allow 30 minutes per 0·5 kg/per 1 lb plus 30 minutes over. For ham allow 20 minutes per 0·5 kg/per 1 lb plus 20 minutes over.

Next prepare the dumplings. Mix all the ingredients together to make a soft dough and shape into 2·5-cm/1-inch balls.

Put the dumplings in the cooking liquid for the last 20 minutes of the calculated cooking time. Make sure that the pan is covered tightly. The dumplings will swell and come to the surface.

Drain the meat and serve surrounded by the dumplings.

Apricot Relish

MAKES 4 (450-g/1-lb) JARS

Any meat left over on the boiled beef or ham joint is delicious served cold. Keep some of this apricot relish in the larder, it stores as well as any chutney. Store it for 1 month before using.

METRIC/IMPERIAL	AMERICAN
450 g/1 lb dried apricots, finely chopped	1 lb dried apricots, finely chopped
675 g/1½ lb onions, finely chopped	1½ lb onions, finely chopped
450 g/1 lb light soft brown sugar	2 cups light soft brown sugar
grated rind and juice of 2 oranges	grated rind and juice of 2 oranges
225 g/8 oz sultanas	1½ cups seedless white raisins
2 teaspoons salt	2 teaspoons salt
1 clove garlic, crushed	1 clove garlic, crushed
2 tablespoons dry mustard	3 tablespoons dry mustard
½ teaspoon ground mixed spice	½ teaspoon ground mixed spice
750 ml/1¼ pints wine vinegar	3 cups wine vinegar

Soak the apricots in enough water to cover overnight. Drain. Put all the ingredients in a large saucepan, bring to the boil stirring until the sugar is dissolved.

Boil, uncovered, stirring frequently, for 1¼ – 1½ hours or until the relish thickens.

Pour into hot sterilised jars and seal.

Curried Beef

SERVES 4

Serve with hot, freshly cooked rice.

METRIC/IMPERIAL	AMERICAN
450 g/1 lb stewing beef	1 lb beef stew meat
1 tablespoon desiccated coconut	1 tablespoon shredded coconut
3 tablespoons water	¼ cup water
2 tablespoons oil	3 tablespoons oil
1 onion, sliced	1 onion, sliced
2 carrots, sliced	2 carrots, sliced
25 g/1 oz plain flour	¼ cup all-purpose flour
1 tablespoon curry powder	1 tablespoon curry powder
600 ml/1 pint beef stock	2½ cups beef stock
1 apple, peeled, cored and diced	1 apple, peeled, cored and diced
2 tablespoons sultanas	3 tablespoons seedless white raisins
1 tablespoon fruit chutney	1 tablespoon fruit chutney
1 clove garlic, crushed	1 clove garlic, crushed
½ teaspoon ground ginger	½ teaspoon ground ginger
salt and pepper	salt and pepper

Cut the beef into cubes. Put the coconut and water into a small saucepan and bring to the boil. Put aside.

Heat the oil in a large saucepan and fry the beef until browned all over. Remove from the pan. Add the onion and carrot and fry until the onion is softened. Stir in the flour and curry powder and cook, stirring continuously, for 5 minutes. Add the stock and the strained liquid from the coconut. Bring to the boil, stirring all the time. Add the fried beef and simmer, covered for 1 hour.

Add the apple, sultanas, chutney, garlic and ginger. Cook for a further 1 hour or until the beef is cooked. Taste and adjust the seasoning.

Serve hot with side dishes of your choice.

Beef and Beer Casserole

SERVES 4

For a really economical and tasty dish, use shin of beef, but this needs long cooking. Otherwise buy chuck steak. Beer helps tenderise the meat.

METRIC/IMPERIAL	AMERICAN
675 g/1½ lb stewing beef	1½ lb beef stew meat
25 g/1 oz plain flour	¼ cup all-purpose flour
salt and pepper	salt and pepper
2 tablespoons oil	3 tablespoons oil
3 onions, chopped	3 onions, chopped
600 ml/1 pint beer	2½ cups beer
½ teaspoon dried mixed herbs	½ teaspoon dried mixed herbs
450 g/1 lb potatoes, cut into 2·5-cm/1-inch chunks	1 lb potatoes, cut into 1-inch chunks

Cut the beef into cubes or ask your butcher to do this for you. Toss in the flour and season well.

Heat the oil in a large saucepan and fry the onion until softened. Add the beef and fry, stirring until browned all over.

Add the beer and herbs. Bring to the boil, stirring and scraping the bottom of the pan all the time. Cover the pan and cook for 1½–2 hours for chuck steak, 2–3 hours for shin. Taste and adjust the seasoning.

Add the potatoes 30 minutes before the cooking time is finished.

Serve from the pan, piping hot.

Swedish Hamburgers

SERVES 6

METRIC/IMPERIAL	AMERICAN
15 g/½ oz margarine	1 tablespoon margarine
1 onion, finely chopped	1 onion, finely chopped
450 g/1 lb minced beef	1 lb ground beef
8 eggs	8 eggs
1 tablespoon chopped capers	1 tablespoon chopped capers
3 tablespoons finely chopped pickled beetroot or chutney	¼ cup finely chopped pickled beets or chutney
salt and pepper	salt and pepper
oil for frying	oil for frying

Melt the margarine in a frying pan and sauté the onion until tender.

Mix the fried onion with the beef. Mix in two of the eggs with the capers, beetroot and seasoning.

Shape the mixture into six round thick patties. Heat a little oil and fry the patties for 5 minutes on each side. Drain and keep hot.

Fry the remaining eggs and place one on each beefburger.

Serve straightaway.

Country Cider Lamb

SERVES 4

METRIC/IMPERIAL	AMERICAN
3 tablespoons oil	$\frac{1}{4}$ cup oil
675–900 g/1$\frac{1}{2}$–2 lb middle neck or scrag end lamb chops	1$\frac{1}{2}$–2 lb lamb neck slices
2 onions, sliced	2 onions, sliced
2 carrots, sliced	2 carrots, sliced
1 turnip, diced	1 turnip, diced
1 tablespoon plain flour	1 tablespoon all-purpose flour
1 clove garlic, crushed (optional)	1 clove garlic, crushed (optional)
2 tomatoes, peeled and sliced	2 tomatoes, peeled and sliced
600 ml/1 pint cider	2$\frac{1}{2}$ cups cider
salt and pepper	salt and pepper

Heat the oil in a large frying pan and brown the pieces of lamb all over. Drain and put in an ovenproof dish. Pour off all but 3 tablespoons of the fat from the pan. Add the onions, carrots and turnip and fry gently for 5–10 minutes. Stir in the flour and cook, stirring for a further 1–2 minutes. Add the garlic, tomatoes and cider and bring to the boil, season to taste then pour over the lamb.

Cook in a moderate oven (180°C, 350°F, Gas Mark 4) for 1–1$\frac{1}{2}$ hours, or until the lamb is tender. Serve hot.

Lamb and Mushroom Hotpot

SERVES 4

METRIC/IMPERIAL	AMERICAN
675 g/1½ lb lamb middle neck chops	1½ lb lamb neck slices
2 lamb's kidneys	2 lamb kidneys
50 g/2 oz plain flour	½ cup all-purpose flour
salt and pepper	salt and pepper
2 tablespoons oil	3 tablespoons oil
450 g/1 lb potatoes, sliced	1 lb potatoes, sliced
450 ml/¾ pint stock	2 cups stock
2 onions, sliced	2 onions, sliced
100 g/4 oz button mushrooms, sliced	¼ lb mushrooms, sliced
chopped parsley to garnish	chopped parsley to garnish

Trim any excess fat from the chops. Cut the kidneys in half, snip out the core and remove the skin. Season the flour well and coat the chops and kidney with it.

Heat the oil in a frying pan and fry the potato lightly. Remove from the pan and drain. Fry the chops and kidney until browned on both sides. Drain and place in an ovenproof casserole.

Pour off all but 1 tablespoon of the fat from the pan and add the remaining flour. Cook, stirring, for 1–2 minutes. Add the stock gradually, stirring all the time, bring to the boil, taste and adjust the seasoning.

Layer the onion and mushrooms on top of the chops and pour the prepared gravy over the top. Cover with a neatly arranged layer of potato.

Cover and cook in a moderate oven (180°C, 350°F, Gas Mark 4) for 1 hour. Remove the cover and cook for a further 20–30 minutes or until the potatoes are browned.

Serve as soon as possible, sprinkled with chopped parsley.

Sweet and Sour Lamb Chops

SERVES 4

The sauce can also be used as a marinade prior to cooking, if you are planning to barbecue the chops.

METRIC/IMPERIAL	AMERICAN
4 lamb chump chops	4 lamb leg chops
1 tablespoon oil	1 tablespoon oil
3 tablespoons vinegar	¼ cup vinegar
3 tablespoons honey	¼ cup honey
1 tablespoon soy sauce	1 tablespoon soy sauce
pinch of ground ginger	dash of ground ginger
salt and pepper	salt and pepper
½ orange, sliced	½ orange, sliced
½ lemon, sliced	½ lemon, sliced

Trim any excess fat from the chops. Heat the oil in a frying pan and brown the chops quickly on both sides.

Transfer the chops to a casserole. Mix together the vinegar, honey, soy sauce, ginger and seasoning. Pour over the chops and scatter the orange and lemon slices on top.

Cover the casserole and cook in a moderate oven (180°C, 350°F, Gas Mark 4) for 30 minutes, or until the chops are tender.

Stuffed Lamb's Hearts

SERVES 4

METRIC/IMPERIAL	AMERICAN
4 large lamb's hearts	4 large lamb hearts
50 g/2 oz plain flour	½ cup all-purpose flour
2 tablespoons oil or dripping	3 tablespoons oil or meat drippings
600 ml/1 pint stock, or half stock and half red wine	2½ cups stock or half stock and half red wine
1 onion, sliced	1 onion, sliced
1 carrot, sliced	1 carrot, sliced
1 bay leaf	1 bay leaf
salt and pepper	salt and pepper
Stuffing:	*Stuffing:*
1 rasher streaky bacon, chopped	1 bacon slice, chopped
100 g/4 oz fresh breadcrumbs	2 cups fresh soft breadcrumbs
1 tablespoon chopped parsley	1 tablespoon chopped parsley
pinch of dried mixed herbs	dash of dried mixed herbs
finely grated rind and juice of 1 lemon	finely grated rind and juice of 1 lemon
50 g/2 oz shredded suet	6 tablespoons chopped suet
salt and pepper	salt and pepper

Prepare the hearts. Wash well under cold running water to remove all the blood. Snip away any sinews and excess fat.

Mix all the stuffing ingredients together. Divide the stuffing into four and stuff the hearts. Secure the hearts closed with small skewers or cocktail sticks.

Coat the hearts in the flour then brown them all over in the oil or dripping. Transfer the hearts to an ovenproof dish. Add any remaining flour to the pan and cook, stirring for 1–2 minutes. Add the stock and bring to the boil, stirring all the time. Taste and adjust the seasoning.

Add the onion, carrot and bay leaf to the dish then cover the hearts and vegetables with the prepared sauce. Cover the dish and cook in a moderate oven (180°C, 350°F, Gas Mark 4) for 1½–2 hours, or until the hearts are very tender.

Baked Liver and Onions

SERVES 4

METRIC/IMPERIAL	AMERICAN
450 g/1 lb lamb's liver	1 lb lamb liver
50 g/2 oz plain flour	½ cup all-purpose flour
salt and pepper	salt and pepper
450 g/1 lb onions, sliced	1 lb onions, sliced
1 tablespoon oil	1 tablespoon oil
stock or red wine to cover	stock or red wine to cover

Cut the liver into thin slices, or ask your butcher to do this for you. Rinse in cold water and pat dry. Season the flour well and use to coat the liver.

Fry the onions in the oil until softened.

Put half the liver in an ovenproof dish, cover with half the onions and cover with the remaining liver and another layer of onions. Add enough stock or red wine to just cover the liver.

Cover the dish and cook in a moderate oven (180°C, 350°F, Gas Mark 4) for 45 minutes.

Serve very hot.

Sausage Hotpot

SERVES 4

METRIC/IMPERIAL	AMERICAN
450 g/1 lb fat pork sausages	1 lb fat pork sausages
1 (227-g/8-oz) packet frozen mixed vegetables, thawed	1 (8-oz) package frozen mixed vegetables, thawed
1 (396-g/14-oz) can tomatoes	1 (14-oz) can tomatoes
2 tablespoons tomato purée	3 tablespoons tomato paste
1 tablespoon Worcestershire sauce	1 tablespoon Worcestershire sauce
750 ml/1¼ pints water or stock	3 cups water or stock
salt and pepper	salt and pepper
450 g/1 lb potatoes	1 lb potatoes
25 g/1 oz butter	2 tablespoons butter

Grill the sausages quickly until browned all over and put in a casserole. Add the mixed vegetables, tomatoes, tomato purée, Worcestershire sauce and water or stock and season to taste. Parboil the potatoes in boiling salted water and cut them in 5-mm/¼-inch slices. Overlap the potatoes on top of the casserole and dot with the butter.

Bake in a moderate oven (180°C, 350°F, Gas Mark 4) for 1 hour or until the sausages are cooked and the potatoes browned.

Serve very hot.

Barbecued Sausages

SERVES 4

METRIC/IMPERIAL	AMERICAN
450 g/1 lb fat pork sausages	1 lb fat pork sausages
1 tablespoon oil	1 tablespoon oil
1 onion, chopped	1 onion, chopped
50 g/2 oz mushrooms, sliced	½ cup mushrooms, sliced
150 ml/¼ pint tomato juice	⅔ cup tomato juice
2 teaspoons cornflour	2 teaspoons cornstarch
1 clove garlic, crushed (optional)	1 clove garlic, crushed (optional)
1 tablespoon soft brown sugar	1 tablespoon soft brown sugar
2 tablespoons malt vinegar	3 tablespoons malt vinegar
few drops of Worcestershire sauce	few drops of Worcestershire sauce
salt and pepper	salt and pepper

Fry the sausages in the oil until browned all over. Drain and pour off all but 1 tablespoon of the fat. Fry the onion until softened then add the mushrooms and cook for 1–2 minutes. Add all the remaining ingredients, whisking well to mix thoroughly. Bring to the boil, stirring, until the sugar is dissolved.

Put the sausages into the sauce and simmer for 15–20 minutes. Serve hot.

Basque Chicken Casserole

SERVES 4

METRIC/IMPERIAL	AMERICAN
1·5 kg/3 lb roasting chicken	3 lb roasting chicken
1 tablespoon oil	1 tablespoon oil
25 g/1 oz butter	2 tablespoons butter
1 onion, thinly sliced	1 onion, thinly sliced
100 g/4 oz button mushrooms, sliced	1 cup mushrooms, sliced
450 g/1 lb tomatoes, peeled and chopped or 1 (396-g/14-oz) can tomatoes	1 lb tomatoes, peeled and chopped or 1 (14-oz) can tomatoes
1 clove garlic, crushed	1 clove garlic, crushed
1 tablespoon lemon juice	1 tablespoon lemon juice
½ teaspoon dried marjoram or oregano	½ teaspoon dried marjoram or oregano
salt and pepper	salt and pepper
300 ml/½ pint stock or 150 ml/¼ pint stock and 150 ml/¼ pint red wine	1¼ cups stock or ⅔ cup stock and ⅔ cup red wine

Cut the chicken into four portions. Heat the oil and butter together in a large saucepan and fry the chicken pieces until browned all over. Remove the chicken and put in an ovenproof casserole. Add the onion to the pan and fry until softened then add all the remaining ingredients.

Bring to the boil then pour over the chicken. Cover the casserole and cook in a moderate oven (180°C, 350°F, Gas Mark 4) for 45 minutes.

Taste and adjust the seasoning then serve piping hot.

Spiced Chicken

SERVES 4

Try serving this chicken on rice, accompanied by a green salad.

METRIC/IMPERIAL	AMERICAN
1·5 kg/3 lb roasting chicken	3 lb roasting chicken
2 tablespoons oil	3 tablespoons oil
1 onion, finely chopped	1 onion, finely chopped
1 stick celery, chopped	1 stalk celery, chopped
1 (227-g/8-oz) can tomatoes	1 (8-oz) can tomatoes
1 teaspoon chilli powder	1 teaspoon chili powder
pinch of ground allspice	dash of ground allspice
1 clove garlic, crushed	1 clove garlic, crushed
150 ml/¼ pint chicken stock	⅔ cup chicken stock
1 tablespoon cornflour	1 tablespoon cornstarch
salt and pepper	salt and pepper

Cut the chicken into four portions. Heat the oil in a large saucepan and fry the chicken portions until browned all over. Remove and place in an ovenproof casserole. Add the onion to the pan and fry until softened. Add the celery, tomatoes, chilli, allspice, garlic, stock and cornflour. Bring to the boil, stirring all the time until slightly thickened then season to taste.

Pour the sauce over the chicken and cover the casserole. Cook in a moderate oven (180°C, 350°F, Gas Mark 4) for 45 minutes. Serve hot.

Country Braised Turkey

SERVES 10

A larger turkey could be used if you have more people to feed.

METRIC/IMPERIAL	AMERICAN
3·5 kg/8 lb turkey	8 lb turkey
salt and pepper	salt and pepper
50 g/2 oz butter	¼ cup butter
1 carrot, sliced	1 carrot, sliced
1 onion, sliced	1 onion, sliced
2 sticks celery, sliced	2 stalks celery, sliced
1 clove garlic, crushed	1 clove garlic, crushed
450 ml/¾ pint stock or dry cider	2 cups stock or dry cider
1 tablespoon cornflour	1 tablespoon cornstarch
apple sauce for serving	applesauce for serving

Wipe the turkey with a damp cloth and season well, inside and out. Truss.

Heat the butter in a saucepan, add the carrot, onion, celery and garlic and fry gently, stirring frequently until softened, about 10–15 minutes.

Put the vegetables in a roasting tin with the stock or cider. Season. Put the turkey on top of the vegetables and cover with a large piece of foil. Cook in a moderately hot oven (190°C, 375°F, Gas Mark 5) for 2¼ hours (allow 15 minutes per 0·5 kg/per 1 lb plus 15 minutes over up to 6·25 kg/14 lb, then 10 minutes per 0·5 kg/per 1 lb over). Remove the foil for the last 30 minutes to brown the turkey.

Put the turkey on a serving plate and keep hot.

Put the vegetables in an electric blender and blend with the cider until smooth. Put into a saucepan. Mix the cornflour with a little water and add to the vegetables. Bring to the boil, stirring all the time. Boil for 1–2 minutes. Taste and adjust the seasoning.

Carve the turkey and serve hot with the sauce. Hand apple sauce separately.

Apple-topped Rabbit with Lemon Butter

SERVES 4

METRIC/IMPERIAL	AMERICAN
4 hindquarter pieces of rabbit	4 hindquarter pieces of rabbit
salt and pepper	salt and pepper
1 onion, sliced	1 onion, sliced
1 carrot, sliced	1 carrot, sliced
1 bay leaf	1 bay leaf
75 g/3 oz butter	6 tablespoons butter
100 g/4 oz fresh breadcrumbs	2 cups fresh soft bread crumbs
1 cooking apple, peeled, cored and grated	1 baking apple, peeled, cored and grated
1 tablespoon chopped parsley	1 tablespoon chopped parsley
2 tablespoons lemon juice	3 tablespoons lemon juice

Put the rabbit in a saucepan with enough water to cover. Season well, add the onion, carrot and bay leaf and bring to the boil. Cover the pan and simmer for 1–2 hours or until the rabbit is cooked. (The time will depend on the age of the rabbit and whether tame or wild.)

Drain the rabbit and put in a shallow ovenproof dish with 150 ml/¼ pint (U.S. ⅔ cup) of the cooking liquid. Melt 50 g/2 oz (U.S. ¼ cup) of the butter and fry the breadcrumbs until crisp. Add the apple, parsley and 1 tablespoon of the lemon juice. Spoon the mixture over the rabbit and cook in a moderately hot oven (200°C, 400°F, Gas Mark 6) for 20 minutes, or until golden.

Soften the remaining butter and beat it with the remaining lemon juice. Serve the rabbit piping hot, topped with the lemon butter.

Cheddar Crumble Fish

SERVES 4

METRIC/IMPERIAL	AMERICAN
450 g/1 lb white fish fillet	1 lb white fish fillet
50 g/2 oz margarine or butter	¼ cup margarine or butter
225 g/8 oz leeks, sliced	½ lb leeks, sliced
25 g/1 oz plain flour	¼ cup all-purpose flour
300 ml/½ pint milk	1¼ cups milk
salt and pepper	salt and pepper
pinch of dry mustard	dash of dry mustard
Cheddar crumble:	*Cheddar crumble:*
175 g/6 oz plain flour	1½ cups all-purpose flour
1 teaspoon dry mustard	1 teaspoon dry mustard
75 g/3 oz margarine or butter	6 tablespoons margarine or butter
100 g/4 oz Cheddar cheese, grated	1 cup grated Cheddar cheese
1 tablespoon chopped parsley	1 tablespoon chopped parsley

Cut the fish into bite-sized pieces.

Melt the margarine or butter in a saucepan and cook the leeks very gently for about 5 minutes, or until softened. Add the flour and milk. Bring to the boil whisking all the time with a balloon whisk. Boil for 1–2 minutes. Add seasoning and mustard to taste.

Put the fish into an ovenproof dish and pour the sauce over the top.

To make the crumble, sift the flour and mustard together into a mixing bowl. Rub in the margarine or butter until the mixture resembles breadcrumbs. Stir in the cheese and parsley.

Spoon the crumble over the fish mixture. Bake in a moderately hot oven (190°C, 375°F, Gas Mark 5) for 20 minutes, or until bubbling and golden.

Serve as soon as possible.

Herring Roes in Batter

SERVES 4–6

This same batter is good for frying white fish fillets in as well. Besides a rich lunch or supper, this dish also makes a lovely but inexpensive meal starter.

METRIC/IMPERIAL	AMERICAN
675 g/1½ lb soft herring roes	1½ lb soft herring roes
salt and pepper	salt and pepper
oil for frying	oil for frying
paprika to garnish	paprika pepper to garnish
horseradish relish for serving	horseradish relish for serving
Batter:	*Batter:*
100 g/4 oz plain flour	1 cup all-purpose flour
salt and pepper	salt and pepper
1 tablespoon oil	1 tablespoon oil
150 ml/¼ pint warm water	⅔ cup warm water
1 egg white	1 egg white

Divide the roes, removing any sinews. Rinse then pat dry and season well.

To make the batter, put the flour in a mixing bowl and season. Add the oil then whisk in the warm water to make a thick smooth batter. Whisk the egg white until stiff and fold into the batter just before using.

Fill a deep frying pan a third to a half full with oil and heat to 180°C/350°F (a 2·5-cm/1-inch cube of bread will brown in about 1 minute).

Dip the roes in the batter and fry until golden and cooked. Drain well then serve sprinkled with paprika. Serve with horseradish relish handed separately.

Soused Mackerel

SERVES 4

This is an inexpensive dish, ideal for serving as a fish salad in summer. The mackerel improve with keeping but should not be kept for longer than 1 week, in the refrigerator.

METRIC/IMPERIAL	AMERICAN
4 medium mackerel	4 medium mackerel
salt and pepper	salt and pepper
300 ml/½ pint malt vinegar	1¼ cups malt vinegar
1 tablespoon mixed whole pickling spice	1 tablespoon mixed whole pickling spice
2 bay leaves	2 bay leaves
1 onion, sliced in rings	1 onion, sliced in rings

Clean, gut and fillet the mackerel, or ask your fishmonger to do this for you. Place skin side down with the tail end towards you and season well. Roll up firmly and place in an ovenproof dish. Pour in the vinegar, add the pickling spice and arrange the bay leaves and onion rings on top.

Cover the dish and cook in a moderate oven (160°C, 325°F, Gas Mark 3) for 30 minutes. Cool, then store the fish, still in the liquid, in the refrigerator for 12 hours before serving.

Cottage Cheese and Wholemeal Pancakes

SERVES 6

METRIC/IMPERIAL
Pancakes:
50 g/2 oz wholemeal flour
50 g/2 oz plain flour
1 egg
1 egg yolk
300 ml/½ pint water
salt and pepper
lard for frying
Filling:
25 g/1 oz butter
1 small onion, finely
   chopped
225 g/8 oz cottage cheese
50 g/2 oz salted peanuts,
   chopped
1 teaspoon dried rosemary,
   crushed

AMERICAN
Pancakes:
½ cup whole meal flour
½ cup all-purpose flour
1 egg
1 egg yolk
1¼ cups water
salt and pepper
shortening for frying
Filling:
2 tablespoons butter
1 small onion, finely
   chopped
½ lb cottage cheese
¼ cup salted peanuts,
   chopped
1 teaspoon dried rosemary,
   crushed

Put the flours in a mixing bowl. Stir in the egg and egg yolk then gradually add the water and seasoning, whisking all the time until the mixture forms a smooth thin batter.

Lightly grease a 15-cm/6-inch frying pan with lard and heat until the lard begins to smoke a little. Add 2 tablespoons of the batter and tilt the pan so that it is just evenly covered. Cook until lightly browned underneath then flip the pancake over and cook the other side until browned. Put on a plate and keep hot while you cook the rest of the pancakes. Stack them, one on top of the other.

Next, make the filling. Heat the butter in a saucepan and fry the onion until softened. Stir in the remaining filling ingredients and season well.

Divide the filling equally between the pancakes and roll up. Put the pancakes close together in a single layer in an ovenproof dish. Cover with foil and reheat if necessary in a moderately hot oven (190°C, 375°F, Gas Mark 5) for 15–20 minutes. Serve as soon as possible.

Glamorgan Sausages

SERVES 4–6

A very economical and tasty meal.

METRIC/IMPERIAL	AMERICAN
1 onion, grated or very finely chopped	1 onion, grated or very finely chopped
175 g/6 oz Cheddar cheese, grated	1½ cups grated Cheddar cheese
275 g/10 oz fresh breadcrumbs	5 cups fresh soft bread crumbs
pinch of dried sage	dash of dried sage
pinch of dry mustard	dash of dry mustard
2 eggs, separated	2 eggs, separated
salt and pepper	salt and pepper
fresh breadcrumbs for coating	fresh breadcrumbs for coating
oil for frying	oil for frying

Mix the onion, cheese, breadcrumbs, sage, mustard, egg yolks and seasoning thoroughly.

Divide the mixture into 12 and roll each portion into a small sausage shape.

Coat each sausage in egg white then press on a coating of breadcrumbs.

Heat about 1 cm/2·5 inches oil in a frying pan. Fry the sausages until golden all over, turning once, for 5–7 minutes. Drain on absorbent kitchen paper.

Serve as soon as possible.

Dishes for Entertaining

There is one basic rule when you entertain: make sure that you have tried the dishes before and know they will be enjoyed. Choose dishes that are suitable to the occasion. 'Entertaining' does not just mean a grand dinner party. Suppers, lunches, barbecues and so on, all come under this heading if guests are coming. The guests also can vary – they may be good friends, or perhaps business acquaintances whom you hardly know.

Follow a few helpful pointers for a successful occasion:

★Give yourself plenty of time to plan ahead, at least a week would be ideal.

★Choose a main dish and build the rest of your menu around it. Keep a good balance of flavour, texture and colour. A meal that has not got enough variation in one or all of these will be very boring.

★Plan a menu with some dishes that can be prepared entirely in advance to avoid too much last minute finishing off.

★Make a shopping list.

★Plan your cooking timetable. This could be just a mental note or you could actually write it down so that nothing is forgotten. Check the recipes for the time involved in preparation and cooking.

★Do not forget to garnish the dishes attractively before bringing them to the table.

A well-planned and well-prepared meal will be enjoyed by everyone, especially the hostess.

Hunter's Leg of Lamb

SERVES 8 – 10

Start this recipe a few days before you need to serve it.

METRIC/IMPERIAL	AMERICAN
1·75 kg/4 lb leg of lamb	4 lb leg of lamb
1·15 litres/2 pints dry red wine	5 cups dry red wine
2 tablespoons olive oil	3 tablespoons olive oil
2 tablespoons red wine vinegar	3 tablespoons red wine vinegar
2 carrots, sliced	2 carrots, sliced
1 onion, sliced	1 onion, sliced
8 peppercorns	8 peppercorns
6 cloves	6 cloves
1 bouquet garni	1 bouquet garni
salt and pepper	salt and pepper
6 rashers streaky bacon	6 bacon slices
100 g/4 oz redcurrant jelly	⅓ cup redcurrant jelly

Wipe the leg of lamb and put it in a large glass or ceramic bowl. Mix together the wine, oil, vinegar, carrot, onion, peppercorns, cloves, bouquet garni and seasoning. Pour over the lamb, cover and leave in a cool place for 3 or 4 days, turning the lamb over occasionally.

Put the lamb in a roasting tin with the marinade and arrange the bacon rashers over the top. Roast in a moderate oven (180°C, 350°F, Gas Mark 4) for about 1 hour 40 minutes (allowing 20 minutes per 0·5 kg/per 1 lb plus 20 minutes over). Baste frequently with the marinade.

Put the lamb on a serving dish, remove the bacon rashers and keep hot.

Strain the cooking liquid and any remaining marinade into a saucepan. Bring to the boil and boil rapidly, uncovered, until reduced by half. Add the redcurrant jelly and stir until dissolved. Taste and adjust the seasoning.

Pour a little sauce over the meat and serve the rest separately.

Roasting Time Table

Beef	*Serve with horseradish sauce and Yorkshire pudding.*
	180°C, 350°F, Gas Mark 4
underdone	15 minutes per 0·5 kg/per 1 lb plus 15 minutes over.
medium	20 minutes per 0·5 kg/per 1 lb plus 20 minutes over.
well done	25 minutes per 0·5 kg/per 1 lb plus 25 minutes over.
Lamb	*Serve with mint sauce, onion sauce or redcurrant jelly.*
	180°C, 350°F, Gas Mark 4
pink	20 minutes per 0·5 kg/per 1 lb plus 20 minutes over.
well done	30 minutes per 0·5 kg/per 1 lb plus 30 minutes over.
Pork	*Serve with apple sauce and sage and onion stuffing.*
	230°C, 450°F, Gas Mark 8 30 minutes per 0·5 kg/per 1 lb plus 30 minutes over. then 180°C, 350°F, Gas Mark 4 Cook at the high temperature for 30 minutes then reduce the temperature for the remaining time.
Chicken	*Serve with bread sauce or parsley and thyme stuffing.*
	180°C, 350°F, Gas Mark 4 Allow 20 minutes per 0·5 kg/per 1 lb plus 20 minutes over.
Turkey	*Serve with bread sauce, small sausages, bacon rolls and sage and onion stuffing.*
	180°C, 350°F, Gas Mark 4 Allow 15 minutes per 0·5 kg/per 1 lb up to 6·25 kg/14 lb and 10 minutes for every 0·5 kg/1 lb over 6·25 kg/14 lb.
Duck	*Serve with orange sauce and sage and onion stuffing.*
	190°C, 375°F, Gas Mark 5 Allow 25 minutes per 0·5 kg/per 1 lb and 5 minutes over.

Grilling Time Table

Cook meat under a hot grill. Reduce the temperature to cook it through or move the meat away from the source of heat so that it does not burn.

Steak (2·5 cm/1 inch thick)
rare 4 minutes each side, including sealing the outside.
medium 4 – 5 minutes each side, including
cooked sealing the outside.
well done 7 minutes each side, including sealing the outside.

Lamb 15 – 20 minutes total cooking time.
chops 10 minutes total cooking time.
cutlets

Pork 20 – 25 minutes total cooking time.
loin or spare
rib chops

Chicken 20 – 25 minutes total cooking time,
quarters push a sharp knife into the thickest part – no pink juices should come out.

Lamb Cutlets

SERVES 4

Lamb cutlets make an elegant dish to serve when entertaining. They are quick and easy to prepare and cook. They are also very adaptable and can be served in so many ways depending on the occasion. Cutlets can vary a lot in quality, so buy from a reliable butcher.

METRIC/IMPERIAL	AMERICAN
8 best end of neck cutlets	8 rib lamb chops
sauce (see right)	sauce (see right)
1 tablespoon oil	1 tablespoon oil
25 g/1 oz butter	2 tablespoons butter
salt and pepper	salt and pepper
8 cutlet frills (optional)	8 cutlet frills (optional)

Trim the excess fat from the cutlets and scrape the meat off the end 2·5 cm/1 inch of bone.

Make the sauce or marinade of your choice.

Heat the oil and butter together in a large frying pan and brown the cutlets quickly on both sides. Reduce the heat and cook until tender, turning once more. The total cooking time will be about 10 minutes but will vary according to the thickness of the cutlets and to how you like your lamb cooked. Season well.

Add the sauce and put the cutlet frills on the bones.

Port Sauce

METRIC/IMPERIAL	AMERICAN
1 teaspoon French mustard	1 teaspoon French mustard
few drops of Worcestershire sauce	few drops of Worcestershire sauce
3 tablespoons port	$\frac{1}{4}$ cup port
1 teaspoon cornflour	1 teaspoon cornstarch
150 ml/$\frac{1}{4}$ pint whipping cream	$\frac{2}{3}$ cup whipping cream
salt and pepper	salt and pepper

Put all the ingredients into a saucepan and bring slowly to the boil, stirring all the time. Simmer very gently for 1–2 minutes.

Pour a little sauce over the cutlets and serve the rest separately.

Provençale Sauce

METRIC/IMPERIAL	AMERICAN
2 tablespoons olive oil	3 tablespoons olive oil
900 g/2 lb red ripe tomatoes, peeled and chopped	2 lb red ripe tomatoes, peeled and chopped
1 clove garlic, crushed	1 clove garlic, crushed
1 onion, finely chopped	1 onion, finely chopped
1 stick celery, finely chopped	1 stalk celery, finely chopped
1 bouquet garni	1 bouquet garni
pinch of sugar	dash of sugar
salt and pepper	salt and pepper

Heat the olive oil in a saucepan. Add the remaining ingredients and heat until bubbling, stirring all the time. Cook, stirring occasionally, for 30 minutes, or until soft and pulpy. Adjust the seasoning and remove the bouquet garni.

Cider Braised Pork

SERVES 6–8

Choose fillet end of pork leg or, for economy, a blade or spare rib joint. Use onions or celery if leeks are out of season.

METRIC/IMPERIAL	AMERICAN
1·5 kg/3 lb joint of pork	3 lb joint of pork
450 g/1 lb leeks, sliced	1 lb leeks, sliced
675 g/1½ lb potatoes, thinly sliced	1½ lb potatoes, thinly sliced
2 apples, peeled and sliced	2 apples, peeled and sliced
salt and pepper	salt and pepper
600 ml/1 pint dry cider	2½ cups dry cider
50 g/2 oz butter	¼ cup butter

Wipe the pork with a damp cloth.

Put a layer of leeks in the bottom of a roasting tin and arrange the potatoes on top. Scatter the apple slices over the top. Season well.

Place the pork on top of the apples and pour over the cider. Dot the apples and vegetables with butter.

Roast in a moderate oven (180°C, 350°F, Gas Mark 4) for 2 hours, or until the pork is tender and the vegetables browned. Cover the vegetables if they brown too quickly.

Serve straight from the pan – the vegetables are delicious.

Provençale Beef Stew

SERVES 4–6

METRIC/IMPERIAL	AMERICAN
1 kg/2 lb chuck steak	2 lb chuck steak
300 ml/½ pint red wine	1¼ cups red wine
3 tablespoons olive oil	¼ cup olive oil
1 bouquet garni	1 bouquet garni
thin strip orange rind	thin strip orange rind
2 rashers streaky bacon, chopped	2 bacon slices, chopped
2 carrots, thinly sliced	2 carrots, thinly sliced
2 onions, thinly sliced	2 onions, thinly sliced
50 g/2 oz button mushrooms	½ cup mushrooms
1 (227-g/8-oz) can tomatoes	1 (8-oz) can tomatoes
2 cloves garlic, crushed	2 cloves garlic, crushed
1 tablespoon chopped parsley	1 tablespoon chopped parsley
salt and pepper	salt and pepper
300 ml/½ pint beef stock	1¼ cups beef stock
12 black olives, stoned	12 ripe olives, pitted

Cut the beef into bite-sized pieces, or ask your butcher to do this. Put it in a bowl with the wine and leave for at least 2 hours, preferably overnight.

Put the meat, marinade and all the remaining ingredients, except the olives, in a saucepan. Bring to the boil then cover and simmer gently for 1½–2 hours, or until the meat is tender. Add the olives 30 minutes before the cooking time is completed. Discard the bouquet garni and orange rind and serve the stew piping hot.

Kebabs

Kebabs are an import from the East. Different countries have their own variations, but basically they are pieces of meat, usually lamb or beef, threaded on skewers. The meat is usually marinated before cooking to help tenderise it and add flavour. Frequently vegetables are threaded on to the skewers between the pieces of meat. They are lovely for informal meals when entertaining, served with rice. They are also ideal barbecue fare – serve them with crusty French bread. Salads are the ideal accompaniment and altogether they make a very simple to prepare meal.

METRIC/IMPERIAL	AMERICAN
900 g/2 lb rump or topside steak or lean boneless leg of lamb	2 lb beef round or rump steak or boneless leg of lamb
marinade (see right)	marinade (see right)
8 small onions	8 small onions
1 green pepper, cut in 2·5-cm/1-inch squares	1 green pepper, cut in 1-inch squares
4 small tomatoes, halved	4 small tomatoes, halved
8 bay leaves	8 bay leaves
salt and pepper	salt and pepper

Cut the meat into neat 2·5-cm/1-inch cubes. Put into the prepared marinade and leave for 3 – 4 hours.

Drain the meat and thread on to four long skewers alternating with the vegetables and bay leaves. Season well. Cook under a moderately hot grill or over a charcoal barbecue for 10 – 15 minutes or until the meat is tender. Turn the kebabs frequently and baste with the remaining marinade.

Shish Kebabs

METRIC/IMPERIAL	AMERICAN
150 ml/¼ pint olive oil	⅔ cup olive oil
150 ml/¼ pint red wine	⅔ cup red wine
2 teaspoons salt	2 teaspoons salt
1 teaspoon black pepper	1 teaspoon black pepper
1 teaspoon ground cinnamon	1 teaspoon ground cinnamon

Put all the ingredients in a screw-top jar. Shake vigorously until well mixed then pour over the meat. Stir the meat frequently.

Greek Kebabs

METRIC/IMPERIAL	AMERICAN
150 ml/¼ pint olive oil	⅔ cup olive oil
juice of 1 lemon	juice of 1 lemon
2 teaspoons chopped marjoram	2 teaspoons chopped marjoram
salt and pepper	salt and pepper

Put all the ingredients into a screw-top jar. Shake vigorously until well mixed then pour over the meat. Stir the meat frequently.

Tandoori Marinade

METRIC/IMPERIAL	AMERICAN
1 (142-ml/5-fl oz) carton natural yoghurt	1 (5-fl oz) carton plain yogurt
1 small onion, finely chopped or grated	1 small onion, finely chopped or grated
1 teaspoon ground cinnamon	½ teaspoon ground cinnamon
1 teaspoon salt	1 teaspoon salt
½ teaspoon ground cardamom	½ teaspoon ground cardamom
½ teaspoon ground black pepper	½ teaspoon ground black pepper
¼ teaspoon ground cumin	¼ teaspoon ground cumin
¼ teaspoon ground cloves	¼ teaspoon ground cloves
¼ teaspoon ground coriander	¼ teaspoon ground coriander
¼ teaspoon ground ginger	¼ teaspoon ground ginger
2 tablespoons oil	3 tablespoons oil
1 tablespoon lemon juice	1 tablespoon lemon juice

Mix all the ingredients together in a large bowl. Stir in the meat and marinate for at least 2 hours.

Tomato Sauce

Serve this sauce with the kebabs if liked. A variation on the kebabs is to thread just meat and onion on to the skewers then serve coated in this tomato and pepper sauce.

METRIC/IMPERIAL	AMERICAN
2 tablespoons olive oil	3 tablespoons olive oil
1 onion, finely chopped	1 onion, finely chopped
1 green pepper, finely chopped	1 green pepper, finely chopped
1 clove garlic, crushed	1 clove garlic, crushed
4 red ripe tomatoes, peeled and chopped	4 red ripe tomatoes, peeled and chopped
2 tablespoons tomato purée	3 tablespoons tomato paste
2 teaspoons paprika	2 teaspoons paprika pepper
salt and pepper	salt and pepper

Heat the oil in a saucepan and fry the onions and pepper until softened. Add all the remaining ingredients with 4 tablespoons (U.S. ⅓ cup) water. Bring to the boil then cook gently for about 15 minutes, or until soft and pulpy. Serve hot.

Soured Pork with Mushrooms

SERVES 4

METRIC/IMPERIAL	AMERICAN
450 g/1 lb pork fillet, very thinly sliced	1 lb pork tenderloin, very thinly sliced
175 g/6 oz salted biscuits or dry bread	6 oz salted crackers or dry bread
2 (142-ml/5-fl oz) cartons soured cream	2 (5-fl oz) cartons dairy sour cream
1 egg	1 egg
salt and pepper	salt and pepper
50 g/2 oz butter	¼ cup butter
2 tablespoons oil	3 tablespoons oil
100 g/4 oz mushrooms, sliced	¼ lb mushrooms, sliced
150 ml/¼ pint white wine	⅔ cup white wine
pinch of grated nutmeg	dash of grated nutmeg

Pound the slices of pork with a meat mallet until as thin as possible. Crush the biscuits into fine crumbs (an electric blender is good for this). Beat half the soured cream with the egg and seasoning. Coat the pork in the egg mixture then in the crumbs.

Heat the butter and oil in a large frying pan. Fry the pork for 3 minutes on each side, or until cooked and golden. Keep hot. Add the mushrooms and cook for 2 minutes. Stir in the wine and boil for 2 – 3 minutes. Stir in the remaining soured cream and the nutmeg. Reheat without boiling. Adjust the seasoning, pour over the pork and serve as soon as possible.

Veal Tiffany

SERVES 4

Ready prepared cream cheese is ideal for this.

METRIC/IMPERIAL	AMERICAN
8 thin (75-g/3-oz) slices veal	8 thin (3-oz) slices veal
salt and pepper	salt and pepper
225 g/8 oz garlic or herb-flavoured cream cheese	½ lb garlic or herb-flavored cream cheese
2 eggs, beaten	2 eggs, beaten
dry breadcrumbs for coating	dry bread crumbs for coating
oil for frying	oil for frying

Ask your butcher to cut the veal as thinly as possible.

Season the veal then put an eighth of the cream cheese on each slice. Roll up the slices, tucking in the sides to enclose the cream cheese.

Beat the eggs together on a plate, put the breadcrumbs on another plate. Coat the veal rolls in beaten egg then in breadcrumbs, pressing the coating on firmly. Repeat the egg and breadcrumb process so that each roll has a thick double coating.

Chill the rolls for at least 1 hour.

Heat the oil for deep frying to 180°C/350°F (a 2·5-cm/1-inch cube of bread will brown in 1 minute).

Fry the veal rolls until golden and cooked through. Drain well on absorbent kitchen paper and serve immediately.

Glazed Bacon or Ham

SERVES 6–8

Bacon makes a lovely dish for entertaining. Serve it throughout the year, not just with the turkey at Christmas. Try baking it with one of these glazes which can also be used with ready cooked and canned hams.

METRIC/IMPERIAL	AMERICAN
1·5–1·75 kg/3–4 lb bacon joint	3–4 lb bacon joint
1 onion	1 onion
1 carrot	1 carrot
1 bay leaf	1 bay leaf
cloves	cloves
glaze (see opposite)	glaze (see opposite)

Put the bacon in a large saucepan with enough cold water to cover. Bring to the boil then drain. Cover with fresh cold water, add the onion, carrot and bay leaf and bring to the boil. Cover the pan and simmer gently until cooked. Allow 20 minutes per 0·5 kg/per 1 lb.

Drain and cool slightly. Carefully ease the skin away from the fat using a sharp knife.

Put the bacon in a roasting tin and score the fat in a lattice pattern. Where the lattice crosses, stud with a clove. Pour the chosen glaze over the bacon fat and roast in a moderate oven (180°C, 350°F, Gas Mark 4) for 20–30 minutes, or until browned.

Serve straightaway or leave until completely cold before serving.

Cherry Glaze

METRIC/IMPERIAL	AMERICAN
4 tablespoons black cherry preserve	⅓ cup bing cherry preserve
1 tablespoon brandy (optional)	1 tablespoon brandy (optional)
1 teaspoon cornflour	1 teaspoon cornstarch
canned black cherries to garnish	canned bing cherries to garnish

Mix all the ingredients together in a saucepan. Heat gently until bubbling then spread over the bacon fat and bake.

Heat some black cherries round the ham as it cooks and serve as a garnish.

Burgundy Orange Glaze

METRIC/IMPERIAL	AMERICAN
4 tablespoons red wine	⅓ cup red wine
50 g/2 oz soft brown sugar	¼ cup soft brown sugar
2 tablespoons orange marmalade	3 tablespoons orange marmalade
slices of orange to garnish	slices of orange to garnish

Put the wine, sugar and marmalade into a saucepan and bring to the boil. Simmer 1–2 minutes. Pour the glaze over the bacon and bake. Heat some orange slices round the bacon as it cooks and serve as a garnish.

Pineapple Glaze

METRIC/IMPERIAL
4 tablespoons pineapple
  juice
50 g/2 oz soft brown sugar
pinch of ground cinnamon
canned pineapple rings to
  garnish

AMERICAN
⅓ cup pineapple juice
¼ cup soft brown sugar
dash of ground cinnamon
canned pineapple rings to
  garnish

Mix the juice with the brown sugar and cinnamon.
Spread over the bacon and bake. Heat some pineapple
rings round the bacon as it cooks and serve as a garnish.

Treacle Glaze

METRIC/IMPERIAL
2 tablespoons black treacle
2 tablespoons orange juice
2 teaspoons dry mustard

AMERICAN
3 tablespoons molasses
3 tablespoons orange juice
2 teaspoons dry mustard

Mix all the ingredients together in a saucepan until
runny and well combined. Pour over the bacon before
baking.

Glazed Chicken Jamboree

SERVES 4

This glaze is also good for brushing over chicken pieces while barbecuing.

METRIC/IMPERIAL	AMERICAN
1·5 kg/3 lb roasting chicken	3 lb roasting chicken
1 onion, halved	1 onion, halved
1 orange, quartered	1 orange, quartered
salt and pepper	salt and pepper
pinch of curry powder	dash of curry powder
Glaze:	*Glaze:*
50 g/2 oz seedless raisins	⅓ cup seeded raisins
1 tablespoon wine vinegar	1 tablespoon wine vinegar
1 tablespoon honey	1 tablespoon honey
3 tablespoons redcurrant jelly	¼ cup redcurrant jelly
3 tablespoons fruit chutney	¼ cup fruit chutney

Cut the chicken into four portions, place the onion and orange in a roasting tin and place the chicken portions on top. Season and rub the chicken with the curry powder. Roast in a moderate oven (180°C, 350°F, Gas Mark 4) for 15 minutes.

Meanwhile, put all the glaze ingredients in a saucepan and heat gently, stirring until well mixed.

Spoon a little glaze over the chicken. Roast for a further 20–30 minutes or until cooked, basting occasionally with the glaze and the dripping in the roasting tin.

Serve hot with any remaining glaze.

Coconut Cream Chicken

SERVES 4

This is a Thai dish. Serve it with rice and a variety of side dishes – sliced banana in lemon juice, diced cucumber in yogurt, sliced tomato in French dressing, mango chutney, peanuts and so on.

METRIC/IMPERIAL	AMERICAN
1·5 kg/3 lb chicken	3 lb chicken
50 g/2 oz desiccated coconut	⅔ cup shredded coconut
600 ml/1 pint single cream	2½ cups light cream
3 spring onions	3 scallions
2 cloves garlic, crushed	2 cloves garlic, crushed
3 tablespoons peanut butter	¼ cup peanut butter
finely grated rind of 1 lemon	finely grated rind of 1 lemon
1 teaspoon ground coriander	1 teaspoon ground coriander
½ teaspoon chilli powder	½ teaspoon chili powder
1 teaspoon sugar	1 teaspoon sugar
1 teaspoon salt	1 teaspoon salt
50g/2 oz butter	¼ cup butter
1 tablespoon soy sauce	1 tablespoon soy sauce

Chop the chicken into eight portions. Put the coconut into a bowl, heat the cream until bubbles begin to rise and pour on to the coconut. Put aside until cold then strain, pressing the coconut well to extract all the liquid.

Grind the spring onions, garlic, peanut butter, lemon rind, coriander, chilli, sugar and salt together with a pestle and mortar or in an electric blender.

Coat the chicken pieces in the ground mixture. Heat the butter in a large frying pan and fry the chicken until browned. Add the coconut flavoured cream and soy sauce. Bring to the boil and simmer for 30 minutes or until the chicken is tender. Serve hot.

St. Clements Duck

SERVES 4

METRIC/IMPERIAL	AMERICAN
2·5–3 kg/5½–6½ lb duck	5½–6½ lb duck
salt and pepper	salt and pepper
grated rind and juice of 1 orange	grated rind and juice of 1 orange
grated rind and juice of 1 lemon	grated rind and juice of 1 lemon
2 sticks celery, chopped	2 stalks celery, chopped
2 cloves garlic, crushed	2 cloves garlic, crushed
50 g/2 oz butter	¼ cup butter
300 ml/½ pint white wine	1¼ cups white wine
300 ml/½ pint chicken stock (from giblets)	1¼ cups chicken stock (from giblets)
2 egg yolks	2 egg yolks
orange segments and sprigs of mint to garnish	orange segments and sprigs of mint to garnish

Season the duck well inside and out. Rub half the orange and lemon rind all over the outside of the duck. Squeeze the fruit juice and put half of the remaining orange and lemon rind inside the bird with the celery, garlic and half the butter.

Put the duck on a rack over a roasting tin. Pour the wine into the pan and roast the duck in a moderately hot oven (190°C, 375°F, Gas Mark 5) for 25 minutes per 0·5 kg/per 1 lb plus 25 minutes over.

Cut the duck into eight pieces and put them on a serving plate.

Skim the fat from the roasting tin. Strain the cooking juices into a saucepan and add the stock. Bring to the boil and boil rapidly for 3 minutes. Mix the egg yolks with the orange and lemon juice. Stir into the sauce and reheat without boiling. Whisk in the remaining butter, a few small pieces at a time. Heat gently without boiling. Taste and adjust the seasoning. Pour the sauce over the duck and serve, garnished with orange segments and sprigs of mint.

Pheasant with Pâté Cream Sauce

SERVES 3 – 4

METRIC/IMPERIAL	AMERICAN
1 – 1·25 kg/2 – 2½ lb pheasant or guinea fowl	2 – 2½ lb pheasant or guinea fowl
50 g/2 oz butter	¼ cup butter
1 onion, chopped	1 onion, chopped
100 g/4 oz liver pâté	¼ lb liver pâté
2 teaspoons paprika	2 teaspoons paprika pepper
salt and pepper	salt and pepper
4 rashers streaky bacon	4 bacon slices
2 tablespoons brandy	3 tablespoons brandy
150 ml/¼ pint double cream	⅔ cup heavy cream

Prepare the pheasant or guinea fowl for roasting. Melt the butter in a saucepan and fry the onion until softened. Cut the pâté in small pieces and add to the pan with paprika and seasoning. Fry, stirring, until lightly browned.

Put half the pâté mixture inside the bird and truss. Place the bacon rashers over the bird.

Roast in a moderate oven (180°C, 350°F, Gas Mark 4) for 1 – 2 hours according to the age of the bird.

Heat the remaining pâté mixture, add the brandy and ignite. Pour the cream over the flames. Reheat, without boiling, stirring all the time. Strain then taste and season.

Cut the bird into six or eight pieces and serve with a spoonful of the stuffing. Serve the sauce separately.

Pigeons with Orange and Rice Stuffing

SERVES 4

METRIC/IMPERIAL	AMERICAN
4 pigeons	4 pigeons
100 g/4 oz butter	½ cup butter
1 large onion, chopped	1 large onion, chopped
1 stick celery, chopped	1 stalk celery, chopped
100 g/4 oz cooked long-grain rice	⅔ cup cooked long-grain rice
1 teaspoon chopped mint	1 teaspoon chopped mint
1 teaspoon chopped parsley	1 teaspoon chopped parsley
salt and pepper	salt and pepper
2 large oranges	2 large oranges
3 tablespoons sherry	¼ cup sherry
300 ml/½ pint game or chicken stock	1¼ cups game or chicken stock
4 rashers streaky bacon	4 bacon slices

Prepare the pigeons. If the giblets are available, reserve the liver and boil the remainder for 30 minutes to make stock.

Heat half of the butter and fry the onion until softened. Chop the reserved livers and add with the celery, rice, mint, parsley, seasoning and the grated rind of ½ orange.

Stuff the pigeons with the rice stuffing. Melt the remaining butter in a large pan and fry the pigeons until browned all over. Add the sherry and stock, and arrange a rasher of bacon over each pigeon. Cover and cook until the pigeons are tender. Wild pigeons will take 1½ – 2 hours.

Peel the oranges and divide into segments, removing all the skin and pith. Add the segments, with any juice, to the pan and cook for a further 10 minutes. Serve hot.

Sole and Mushroom au Gratin

SERVES 4

Most flat fish can be used for this recipe – choose one to fit your budget. Dover sole are lovely but very expensive, witch soles are comparatively cheap and are still very good.

METRIC/IMPERIAL	AMERICAN
4 small sole (Dover, lemon, witch or flounder)	4 small sole (lemon, witch or flounder)
salt and pepper	salt and pepper
1 tablespoon lemon juice	1 tablespoon lemon juice
100 g/4 oz mushrooms, chopped	$\frac{1}{4}$ lb mushrooms, chopped
1 onion, finely chopped	1 onion, finely chopped
2 tablespoons chopped parsley	3 tablespoons chopped parsley
100 g/4 oz fresh breadcrumbs	2 cups fresh soft bread crumbs
50 g/2 oz butter, melted	$\frac{1}{4}$ cup butter, melted
wedges of lemon to garnish	wedges of lemon to garnish

Clean and skin the fish, or ask your fishmonger to do this for you. Rinse in cold water and pat dry. Make two cuts across the centre on each side at the thickest part. Season well and sprinkle with the lemon juice.

Mix the mushrooms with the onion and parsley. Spread half the mixture in a well buttered ovenproof dish, place the sole on top and cover with the remaining mixture.

Press the breadcrumbs over the top and drizzle the butter over the surface.

Bake in a moderately hot oven (190°C, 375°F, Gas Mark 5) for 30 minutes, or until the fish is cooked and the breadcrumbs browned. Serve on individual plates, garnished with a wedge of lemon.

Fillets of Plaice Mornay

SERVES 4

An ideal choice for the fish course of a dinner party.

METRIC/IMPERIAL	AMERICAN
2 large plaice, skinned and filleted	2 large plaice, skinned and filleted
1 small carrot, sliced	1 small carrot, sliced
1 small onion, sliced	1 small onion, sliced
1 bay leaf	1 bay leaf
2 tablespoons white wine	3 tablespoons white wine
thin slice of lemon	thin slice of lemon
salt and pepper	salt and pepper
chopped parsley to garnish	chopped parsley to garnish
Sauce:	*Sauce:*
25 g/1 oz butter	2 tablespoons butter
25 g/1 oz plain flour	$\frac{1}{4}$ cup all-purpose flour
150 ml/$\frac{1}{4}$ pint milk	$\frac{2}{3}$ cup milk
25 g/1 oz Cheddar cheese, grated	$\frac{1}{2}$ cup grated Cheddar cheese
50 g/2 oz grated Parmesan cheese	$\frac{1}{2}$ cup grated Parmesan cheese
salt and pepper	salt and pepper
pinch of dry mustard	dash of dry mustard

Wash and trim the fillets. If you have double fillets (the full width of the fish), cut them down the centre to make thin fillets. You should have eight thin fillets. Fold the fillets in three and place them in an ovenproof dish. Add the carrot, onion, bay leaf, wine, lemon, seasoning and 1 cm/$\frac{1}{2}$ inch water. Cover and cook in a moderate oven (180°C, 350°F, Gas Mark 4) for 15 minutes, or until the plaice is just cooked.

Meanwhile make the sauce. Put the butter, flour and milk in a saucepan. Bring to the boil, whisking all the time with a balloon whisk. Boil for 1–2 minutes.

Put the cooked fish on a serving plate. Keep hot. Strain the cooking liquid, measure 150 ml/$\frac{1}{4}$ pint (U.S. $\frac{2}{3}$ cup) and whisk it into the sauce with the Cheddar and half the Parmesan. Taste and season with salt, pepper and mustard. Coat the fish evenly with the sauce and sprinkle with the remaining Parmesan. Brown under a hot grill and serve straightaway, sprinkled with chopped parsley.

Halibut Dieppe-style

SERVES 4

When leeks are out of season, try using half a cucumber instead.

METRIC/IMPERIAL	AMERICAN
4 (175-g/6-oz) halibut steaks	4 (6-oz) halibut steaks
salt and pepper	salt and pepper
juice of 1 lemon	juice of 1 lemon
75 g/3 oz butter	6 tablespoons butter
2 leeks, sliced	2 leeks, sliced
1 teaspoon paprika	1 teaspoon paprika pepper
100 g/4 oz peeled prawns	⅔ cup shelled shrimp

Rinse the halibut in cold water, drain then pat dry on absorbent kitchen paper. Put in an ovenproof dish, season well and sprinkle with lemon juice. Dot with 50 g/2 oz (U.S.¼ cup) of the butter, cover and cook in a moderate oven (180°C, 350°F, Gas Mark 4) for 20–30 minutes, or until cooked.

Meanwhile, melt the remaining butter in a saucepan. Add the leeks, cover and cook very gently for 10 minutes, or until softened and tender but not browned. Stir in the paprika and prawns and reheat gently. Season.

Drain the halibut, remove the bones and skin and arrange on a hot serving dish. Spoon the butter, leek and prawn mixture over the top and serve straightaway.

Rice and Pasta

Until recently, rice and pasta have been very popular in other parts of the world, but not so much in this country. Many foreign dishes, particularly from India, China and Italy, would be unthinkable without either rice or pasta as an ingredient or accompanying dish.

They have both been imported into this country for many years now and have recently found a good market mainly as a convenience-style food. We have discovered what good substitutes they make for potatoes – they don't need peeling and cook in half the time. But this is only a tiny bit of the story; rice and pasta open up whole new worlds of cooking. We can now try for ourselves recipes from other countries, such as Italian Cannelloni, Portuguese Chicken and Greek Rice Dolmas, or adapt our own recipes to include them.

Rice used to be sold unprocessed and uncleaned. It is now sold in a form that is quick to prepare and almost foolproof to cook. There are various different types; long-grain rice, which is widely used for most savoury dishes is perhaps the most well known, along with pudding or short-grain rice which is ideal for sweet dishes. Brown rice is unpolished and is not processed at all. Many people prefer the flavour and, as it is nutritionally better for you, it is finding a wide market amongst the diet conscious. Italian risotto rice is also being imported, as is wild rice, which is actually not rice at all but a grass seed. Wild rice is dark brown and the grains long and thin. It has a distinctive flavour but is very expensive, so is not widely sold. Rice can be cooked in many different ways according to its type and the recipe. Follow the instructions on the side of the packet or the recipe you are using.

Pasta is man-made, mainly from wheat flour mixed with oil and water. Egg is sometimes used to enrich it. Sometimes wholemeal flour is used, which makes a brown, less refined pasta which has a nuttier flavour. Pasta is made in so many shapes that it is almost impossible to mention them all here. Enough to say that they come in three general size groups: soup pasta, used for garnishing, such as alphabetti, vermicelli and stars, which take about 5 minutes to cook; medium pasta such as macaroni, shells and spaghetti, which take 10 – 15 minutes to cook and large pasta, such as lasagne and cannelloni, which take 15 – 20 minutes to cook.

Make sure that the water is salted and boiling rapidly. There should be plenty of room for the pasta to move, so use a large saucepan. Rinse the cooked pasta well and stir in a little oil.

Vegetable Lasagne

SERVES 6

A vegetarian dish, or just something a little different for lunch or supper.

METRIC/IMPERIAL	AMERICAN
100 g/4 oz lasagne	¼ lb lasagne
2 tablespoons oil	3 tablespoons oil
225 g/8 oz French beans, chopped	½ lb green beans, chopped
1 leek or onion, thinly sliced	1 leek or onion, thinly sliced
1 (396-g/14-oz) can tomatoes	1 (14-oz) can tomatoes
100 g/4 oz lentils	½ cup lentils
300 ml/½ pint water	1¼ cups water
pinch of oregano	dash of oregano
450 g/1 lb cream or curd cheese	1 lb cream or curd cheese
2 eggs, beaten	2 eggs, beaten
2 tablespoons chopped parsley	3 tablespoons chopped parsley
salt and pepper	salt and pepper
2 tablespoons grated Parmesan cheese	3 tablespoons grated Parmesan cheese

Cook the lasagne in a large saucepan with plenty of boiling salted water for 15-20 minutes or until tender. Drain in a colander and rinse well, separate the pieces and allow to dry.

Heat the oil in a saucepan and fry the beans and leek or onion for 5 minutes, stirring occasionally. Add the tomatoes, lentils, water and oregano. Bring to the boil, then simmer gently for 40 minutes or until the lentils are cooked.

Mix the cream or curd cheese with the eggs and parsley and season well.

Spread half the vegetable mixture in a 1.25-litre/2-pint (U.S. 2½-pint) ovenproof dish and cover with a third of the lasagne. Spread half the cheese mixture over then cover again with lasagne. Add a layer of the remaining vegetable mixture, cover with the remaining lasagne and finally the remaining cheese mixture.

Sprinkle with Parmesan cheese and bake in a moderate oven (180°C, 350°F, Gas Mark 4) for 40 minutes. Serve as soon as possible.

Chicken and Spinach Cannelloni

SERVES 4

METRIC/IMPERIAL	AMERICAN
8 cannelloni shells	8 cannelloni shells
450 ml/¾ pint milk	2 cups milk
1 onion, peeled	1 onion, peeled
1 bay leaf	1 bay leaf
8 cloves	8 cloves
8 peppercorns	8 peppercorns
salt and pepper	salt and pepper
40 g/1½ oz butter	3 tablespoons butter
40 g/1½ oz plain flour	6 tablespoons all-purpose flour
225 g/8 oz cooked chicken, chopped	½ lb cooked chicken chopped
1 (226-g/8-oz) packet frozen spinach, thawed	1 (8-oz) package frozen spinach, thawed
75 g/3 oz Parmesan cheese, grated	¾ cup grated Parmesan cheese

Cook the cannelloni shells in a large saucepan with plenty of boiling salted water for 15-20 minutes or until cooked. Drain well in a colander. Put the milk in a saucepan with the onion, bay leaf, cloves, peppercorns and salt. Bring to the boil then remove the pan from the heat and put aside for 20 minutes. Strain the milk.

Melt the butter in a clean saucepan. Stir in the flour and cook for 1-2 minutes. Gradually mix in the flavoured milk, stirring all the time. Bring to the boil, stirring, and boil for 2-3 minutes. Adjust seasoning if necessary.

Mix the chicken and spinach together with enough sauce to bind. Stuff each cannelloni shell with an eighth of the mixture.

Beat half the cheese into the remaining sauce. Spread a little sauce into an ovenproof dish and arrange the stuffed cannelloni in a single layer on top. Pour over the sauce and sprinkle with the remaining cheese.

Bake in a moderate oven (180°C, 350°F, Gas Mark 4) for 30 minutes or until very hot and golden on top. Serve as soon as possible.

Spaghetti with Chicken Liver Sauce

SERVES 4

METRIC/IMPERIAL	AMERICAN
350 g/12 oz chicken livers	¾ lb chicken livers
2 tablespoons olive oil	3 tablespoons olive oil
2 rashers streaky bacon, chopped	2 bacon slices, chopped
1 clove garlic, crushed (optional)	1 clove garlic, crushed (optional)
1 onion, finely chopped	1 onion, finely chopped
50 g/2 oz mushrooms, sliced	½ cup mushrooms, sliced
2 tablespoons plain flour	3 tablespoons all-purpose flour
3 tablespoons sherry	¼ cup sherry
1 tablespoon tomato purée	1 tablespoon tomato paste
300 ml/½ pint chicken stock	1¼ cups chicken stock
salt and pepper	salt and pepper
350 g/12 oz spaghetti	¾ lb spaghetti

Wash the chicken livers, cut away any sinews and chop finely. Heat half the oil in a saucepan and fry the bacon, garlic and onion for about 10 minutes or until lightly browned. Add the mushrooms and chicken livers and sprinkle in the flour. Cook, stirring for 2 – 3 minutes, or until the chicken liver is lightly coloured.

Add the sherry, tomato purée, stock and seasoning. Bring to the boil then cover and simmer gently for 20 minutes, stirring occasionally.

Meanwhile, cook the spaghetti in a large saucepan of boiling salted water for 15 – 20 minutes, or until just cooked. Drain well in a colander and stir in the remaining olive oil. Serve the spaghetti with the sauce poured over.

Pasta with Aubergine

SERVES 6

A lovely way of serving pasta in a very Italian style.

METRIC/IMPERIAL	AMERICAN
2 large aubergines	2 large eggplants
1 tablespoon salt	1 tablespoon salt
6 tablespoons olive oil	½ cup olive oil
450 g/1 lb curly pasta or shells	1 lb curly pasta or shells
50 g/2 oz Parmesan cheese, grated	½ cup grated Parmesan cheese
Sauce:	*Sauce:*
1 tablespoon olive oil	1 tablespoon olive oil
2 rashers streaky bacon, chopped	2 bacon slices, chopped
1 onion, chopped	1 onion, chopped
1 (396-g/14-oz) can tomatoes or 450 g/1 lb red ripe tomatoes, peeled and chopped	1 (14-oz) can tomatoes or 1 lb red ripe tomatoes, peeled and chopped
3 tablespoons stock or red wine	¼ cup stock or red wine
1 bay leaf	1 bay leaf
pinch of dried thyme	dash of dried thyme
salt and pepper	salt and pepper

Slice the aubergines into 5-mm/¼-inch slices. Sprinkle them with the salt and put aside for 30 minutes. Rinse off the excess salt and drain well. Dry on absorbent kitchen paper. Heat the oil in a frying pan and fry the aubergine slices until golden. Drain well and keep hot.

Cook the pasta in a large saucepan of boiling salted water for 15–20 minutes or until tender. Drain well in a colander and keep hot.

Next make the sauce. Heat the oil in a saucepan and fry the bacon and onion until softened. Add all the remaining ingredients and bring to the boil. Cook, uncovered, for 15–20 minutes or until thickened and pulpy. Taste and adjust the seasoning.

Place the pasta on a heated serving plate, arrange the aubergine on top and pour the sauce over. Serve straightaway with the Parmesan.

Salami Pasta Salad

SERVES 4–6

METRIC/IMPERIAL	AMERICAN
225 g/8 oz salami	½ lb salami
225 g/8 oz pasta shells or other medium sized pasta shapes	½ lb pasta shells or other medium sized pasta shapes
3 tablespoons dry white wine	¼ cup dry white wine
2 tablespoons olive oil	3 tablespoons olive oil
1 head fennel, thinly sliced	1 head fennel, thinly sliced
50 g/2 oz black olives, stoned	⅓ cup ripe olives, pitted
1 tablespoon finely chopped onion	1 tablespoon finely chopped onion
1 clove garlic, crushed	1 clove garlic, crushed
1 tablespoon chopped parsley	1 tablespoon chopped parsley
salt and pepper	salt and pepper
2–3 hard-boiled eggs, quartered	2–3 hard-cooked eggs, quartered

Slice the salami thinly, or ask your delicatessen to do this for you.

Cook the pasta shells in plenty of boiling salted water for 10 minutes, or until tender. Drain well in a colander. Mix lightly with the wine and oil and leave to become completely cold.

In a salad bowl mix together the pasta, fennel and olives. Sprinkle with the onion, garlic and parsley. Season well and toss lightly.

Arrange the salami and hard-boiled egg quarters on top and serve as soon as possible.

Portuguese Chicken with Savoury Rice

SERVES 4

METRIC/IMPERIAL	AMERICAN
1·5 kg/3 lb roasting chicken	3 lb roasting chicken
2 tablespoons oil	3 tablespoons oil
2 onions, chopped	2 onions, chopped
2 carrots, grated	2 carrots, grated
100 g/4 oz garlic sausage, diced	¼ lb garlic sausage, diced
100 g/4 oz bacon, diced	¼ lb bacon, diced
275 g/10 oz long-grain rice	1½ cups long-grain rice
750 ml/1¼ pints water	3 cups water
2 tablespoons finely chopped parsley	3 tablespoons finely chopped parsley
salt and pepper	salt and pepper
4 tablespoons lemon juice	⅓ cup lemon juice
25 g/1 oz butter, melted	2 tablespoons butter, melted
sliced stuffed olives to garnish	sliced stuffed olives to garnish

Cut the chicken into eight portions.

Heat the oil in a flameproof casserole and fry the onion and carrot until softened. Add the garlic sausage, bacon, rice, water and parsley and season well. Bring to the boil and boil for 5 minutes. Arrange the pieces of chicken on top, skin side up. Sprinkle with the lemon juice and melted butter.

Cook, uncovered in a moderately hot oven (200°C, 400°F, Mark 6) for 30–40 minutes. The chicken will be cooked and browned and the rice will have absorbed all the water. Serve as soon as possible, garnished with the olives.

Mushroom Risotto

SERVES 4

This makes a lovely hot first course or an accompaniment for grills and roasts. It can also be used for stuffing vegetables – peppers, aubergines and tomatoes, for instance.

METRIC/IMPERIAL	AMERICAN
2 tablespoons oil	3 tablespoons oil
1 small onion, chopped	1 small onion, chopped
1 clove garlic, crushed	1 clove garlic, crushed
225 g/8 oz long-grain rice	generous 1 cup long-grain rice
100 g/4 oz button mushrooms, sliced	¼ lb mushrooms, sliced
450 ml/¾ pint stock	2 cups stock
150 ml/¼ pint dry white wine	⅔ cup dry white wine
1 tablespoon tomato purée	1 tablespoon tomato paste
salt and pepper	salt and pepper
50 g/2 oz Parmesan cheese, grated	½ cup grated Parmesan cheese
chopped parsley to garnish	chopped parsley to garnish

Heat the oil in a saucepan and fry the onion and garlic until softened. Add the rice and cook until lightly golden. Add the mushrooms, stock, wine, tomato purée and seasoning.

Bring to the boil, stir once then cover the pan and simmer gently for 15–20 minutes, or until the rice is tender and all the liquid is absorbed.

Stir in the cheese with a fork then serve sprinkled liberally with chopped parsley.

77

Lamb Chops with Brown Rice

SERVES 4

METRIC/IMPERIAL	AMERICAN
225 g/8 oz brown rice	generous 1 cup brown rice
salt and pepper	salt and pepper
pinch of dried crushed rosemary	dash of dried crushed rosemary
1 onion, sliced	1 onion, sliced
1 green pepper, sliced	1 green pepper, sliced
2 tomatoes, sliced	2 tomatoes, sliced
4 lamb chump chops	4 lamb leg chops
600 ml/1 pint stock	2½ cups stock

Put the rice in an ovenproof dish. Season and stir in the rosemary. Scatter the onion, pepper and tomatoes over the top and arrange the chops on the vegetables.

Bring the stock to the boil and pour over the chops. Cover and cook in a moderately hot oven (200°C, 400°F, Gas Mark 6) for 20 minutes. Uncover and cook for a further 30 minutes, or until the chops are cooked and the rice is tender. All the liquid should be absorbed. Serve straight from the dish.

Brown Rice Dolmas with Lemon Sauce

SERVES 4

A vegetarian meal at its best. Also good when served as the first course of a meal.

METRIC/IMPERIAL	AMERICAN
600 ml/1 pint stock	$2\frac{1}{2}$ cups stock
150 ml/$\frac{1}{4}$ pint dry white wine	$\frac{2}{3}$ cup dry white wine
1 tablespoon finely chopped onion	1 tablespoon finely chopped onion
salt and pepper	salt and pepper
pinch of dried basil	dash of dried basil
275 g/10 oz brown rice	$1\frac{1}{2}$ cups brown rice
50 g/2 oz Parmesan cheese, grated	$\frac{1}{2}$ cup grated Parmesan cheese
24 large cabbage or vine leaves	24 large cabbage or vine leaves
wedges of lemon to garnish	wedges of lemon to garnish
Sauce:	*Sauce:*
3 eggs	3 eggs
1 tablespoon cornflour	1 tablespoon cornstarch
pinch of salt	dash of salt
300 ml/$\frac{1}{2}$ pint stock	$1\frac{1}{4}$ cups stock
3 tablespoons lemon juice	$\frac{1}{4}$ cup lemon juice

Put the stock, wine, onion, seasoning and basil into a saucepan. Bring to the boil then add the rice. Cover the pan and simmer for 30 minutes. Remove the lid and boil until all the liquid has evaporated and the rice is tender. Cool slightly, then stir in the cheese.

Meanwhile, cook the cabbage or vine leaves in boiling salted water for 2 – 3 minutes, or until soft and pliable. Drain and lay them out flat on the work surface.

Divide the rice mixture between the leaves and roll up, folding in the edges to keep the filling in. Place close together in an ovenproof dish. Add 1 – 2 tablespoons water, cover and reheat in a moderate oven (180°C, 350°F, Gas Mark 4) for 15 – 20 minutes.

Put all the sauce ingredients in a saucepan and cook, whisking all the time with a balloon whisk until just thickened.

Drain the rolls and pour the sauce over. Garnish with the lemon wedges.

Vegetables and Salads

Vegetables and salads are now becoming recognised as an important part of our diet. It is generally understood how important it is to cook them properly so that they look and taste appetising. They can be served as an accompaniment to a meal, as a lovely starter or even as the main dish of the meal. I would not suggest that you become vegetarian without studying the nutritional aspects more fully, but with the price of meat and fish today, a vegetarian dish can replace a meat or fish dish very adequately and cost a fraction of the price.

Choose your greengrocer carefully as it is very easy to buy low quality fruit and vegetables without noticing. Inspect your purchases before buying if possible, but if not, at least before leaving the shop. A good greengrocer will have a high turnover of produce and will buy daily from the market. First class produce does not only taste best but is the most economical; it may cost a little more but in the long run you will have less wastage. Time also destroys vitamins, so the fresher the fruit and vegetables, the better they are for you. If you can grow your own, you get the best, freshest and cheapest fruit and vegetables available.

Root and dried vegetables have the advantage of keeping well, so that they can be stored. If you use a great deal of one variety, buy in bulk then store carefully until needed.

Carrot and Mushroom Loaf

SERVES 4

This loaf can also be made with parsnip or pumpkin. Serve with asparagus sauce.

METRIC/IMPERIAL	AMERICAN
450 g/1 lb carrots	1 lb carrots
40 g/1½ oz butter	3 tablespoons butter
2 teaspoons soft brown sugar	2 teaspoons soft brown sugar
salt and pepper	salt and pepper
300 ml/½ pint stock	1¼ cups stock
100 g/4 oz button mushrooms, sliced	¼ lb mushrooms, sliced
1 small onion, finely chopped	1 small onion, finely chopped
1 tablespoon chopped parsley	1 tablespoon chopped parsley
½ tablespoon chopped fresh dill or ½ teaspoon dried dill	½ tablespoon chopped fresh dill or ½ teaspoon dried dill
3 eggs	3 eggs
25 g/1 oz Cheddar cheese, grated	¼ cup grated Cheddar cheese

Peel the carrots and cut into dice. Heat two-thirds of the butter and fry the carrots until lightly browned. Sprinkle in the sugar and seasoning then add the stock. Cook gently, uncovered, until the carrot is tender and all the liquid evaporated.

Fry the mushrooms and onion in the remaining butter until softened. Stir in the parsley and dill.

Beat the eggs well and fold in the carrot mixture, mushroom mixture and cheese. Put into a 0.5-kg/1-lb loaf tin and stand in a larger tin with warm water halfway up the sides.

Bake in a moderately hot oven (200°C, 400°F, Gas Mark 6) for 30-40 minutes or until firm. Carefully turn the loaf out of the tin and serve hot.

Asparagus Sauce

MAKES ABOUT 300 ml/½ pint (U.S. 1¼ cups)

Serve with grilled meat or carrot and mushroom loaf.

METRIC/IMPERIAL	AMERICAN
1 (283-g/10-oz) can asparagus	1 (10-oz) can asparagus
150 ml/¼ pint stock	⅔ cup stock
salt and pepper	salt and pepper
1 tablespoon soured cream	1 tablespoon dairy sour cream
1 egg yolk	1 egg yolk

Drain the asparagus and blend to a purée in an electric blender. Put in a heatproof bowl with the remaining ingredients. Place over a saucepan of simmering water and cook gently, stirring frequently, until hot and slightly thickened.

Serve as soon as possible.

Beetroot with Orange Sauce

SERVES 4

METRIC/IMPERIAL	AMERICAN
450 g/1 lb cooked beetroot	1 lb cooked beets
1 teaspoon plain flour	1 teaspoon all-purpose flour
25 g/1 oz soft brown sugar	2 tablespoons soft brown sugar
150 ml/¼ pint orange juice	⅔ cup orange juice
1 tablespoon wine vinegar	1 tablespoon wine vinegar
25 g/1 oz butter	2 tablespoons butter
salt and pepper	salt and pepper

Slice the beetroot and arrange in an ovenproof dish. Mix the flour with the sugar, orange juice and vinegar and pour over the beetroot. Dot with butter and season well. Cook in a moderate oven (180°C, 350°F, Gas Mark 4) for 15 minutes. Serve hot with roast poultry or pork.

Celery with Almonds

SERVES 4–6

METRIC/IMPERIAL	AMERICAN
1 small head celery	1 small head celery
50 g/2 oz butter	¼ cup butter
50 g/2 oz flaked almonds	½ cup flaked almonds
salt and pepper	salt and pepper

Scrub the celery until clean. Cut diagonally to make long thin slices.

Heat the butter, add the celery and fry gently, stirring frequently, until almost tender, about 5 minutes. Add the almonds and continue frying until the almonds are lightly browned and the celery is tender but still crisp. Season well and serve as soon as possible.

Broad Beans with Soured Cream

SERVES 4

Other vegetables are also lovely served this way, try mushrooms, carrots, cauliflower or courgettes.

METRIC/IMPERIAL	AMERICAN
450 g/1 lb shelled broad beans	1 lb shelled lima beans
50 g/2 oz butter	¼ cup butter
1 tablespoon plain flour	1 tablespoon all-purpose flour
salt and pepper	salt and pepper
3 tablespoons soured cream	¼ cup dairy sour cream
½ teaspoon grated lemon rind	½ teaspoon grated lemon rind
1 tablespoon chopped parsley	1 tablespoon chopped parsley

Cook the broad beans in boiling salted water for 5–10 minutes or until just tender. Cool slightly then slip off the skins if tough.

Heat the butter in a saucepan, add the beans and sprinkle in the flour. Season well, stir in the soured cream, lemon rind and parsley. Simmer, stirring for 1–2 minutes. Serve straightaway.

Cider Vegetable Hotpot

SERVES 4–6

METRIC/IMPERIAL	AMERICAN
225 g/8 oz swede	½ lb rutabaga
225 g/8 oz turnips	½ lb turnips
75 g/3 oz butter	6 tablespoons butter
2 onions, sliced	2 onions, sliced
2 leeks, sliced	2 leeks, sliced
225 g/8 oz carrots, sliced	½ lb carrots, sliced
40 g/1½ oz plain flour	6 tablespoons all-purpose flour
450 ml/¾ pint dry cider	2 cups dry cider
few drops of Worcestershire sauce	few drops of Worcestershire sauce
1 tablespoon tomato purée	1 tablespoon tomato paste
salt and pepper	salt and pepper
1 teaspoon yeast extract	1 teaspoon yeast extract
450 g/1 lb potatoes, thinly sliced	1 lb potatoes, thinly sliced
oil for brushing	oil for brushing
75 g/3 oz Cheddar cheese, grated	¾ cup grated Cheddar cheese

Cut the swede and turnip into 2·5-cm/1-inch cubes.

Melt the butter in a large saucepan, add the onion, leek, carrot, swede and turnip and fry gently, stirring frequently, for 10 minutes. Remove the vegetables and place them in a lightly greased ovenproof dish.

Put the flour and cider into the saucepan and bring to the boil, whisking all the time with a balloon whisk. Add the Worcestershire sauce, tomato purée, seasoning and yeast extract. Pour the sauce over the vegetables.

Arrange the sliced potato over the vegetables. Brush with oil and sprinkle the cheese on top. Cover and bake in a moderately hot oven (200°C, 400°F, Gas Mark 6) for 1½–2 hours, or until the vegetables are cooked. Uncover for the last 30 minutes to brown the top. Serve as soon as possible.

Cheese Stuffed Courgettes

SERVES 2–4

An accompaniment for grills or a roast dinner, this also makes a vegetarian lunch or supper for two people.

METRIC/IMPERIAL	AMERICAN
4 large courgettes	4 large zucchini
salt and pepper	salt and pepper
100 g/4 oz butter	½ cup butter
1 large onion, finely chopped	1 large onion, finely chopped
1 tablespoon chopped parsley	1 tablespoon chopped parsley
50 g/2 oz Cheddar cheese, grated	½ cup grated Cheddar cheese

Trim the ends from the courgettes and cook whole in a large saucepan of boiling salted water for 15–20 minutes, or until just cooked. Drain.

Cut the courgettes in half lengthways and carefully scoop out the flesh, leaving a thin wall all round. Chop the flesh.

Meanwhile, heat the butter in a saucepan and fry the onion until softened. Add the chopped courgette and cook rapidly until pulpy. Stir in the parsley and half the cheese. Season to taste.

Fill the courgette halves with the mixture and sprinkle the remaining cheese on top. Bake in a moderate oven (180°C, 350°F, Gas Mark 4) for 20 minutes. Serve as soon as possible.

Marrow Casserole

SERVES 4

METRIC/IMPERIAL	AMERICAN
1 small marrow (about 675 g/1½ lb)	1 small zucchini squash (about 1½ lb)
75 g/3 oz butter	6 tablespoons butter
1 onion, chopped	1 onion, chopped
50 g/2 oz Cheddar cheese, grated	½ cup grated Cheddar cheese
salt and pepper	salt and pepper
few drops of Tabasco sauce	few drops of Tabasco sauce
2 eggs, beaten	2 eggs, beaten
2 tomatoes, thinly sliced (optional)	2 tomatoes, thinly sliced (optional)
50 g/2 oz fresh breadcrumbs	1 cup fresh soft bread bread crumbs

Peel the marrow, remove the seeds and cut the flesh into 2-cm/¾-inch cubes.

Heat 50 g/2 oz (U.S. ¼ cup) of the butter in a large saucepan and fry the onion until softened. Remove the pan from the heat and stir in the marrow, cheese, seasoning, Tabasco and eggs. Mix well then put into a greased ovenproof dish. Arrange a layer of tomato on top, if used.

Melt the remaining butter and mix with the breadcrumbs. Press over the vegetables and bake, uncovered, in a moderate oven (160°C, 325°F, Gas Mark 3) for 35 – 40 minutes or until the marrow is just cooked. Serve hot.

Dutch Mackerel Salad

SERVES 4

METRIC/IMPERIAL	AMERICAN
4 smoked mackerel	4 smoked mackerel
2 cooking apples, cored and finely chopped	2 baking apples, cored and finely chopped
1 cooked beetroot, diced	1 cooked beet, diced
1 large cooked potato, diced	1 large cooked potato, diced
1 (142-ml/5-fl oz) carton soured cream	1 (5-fl oz) carton dairy sour cream
salt and pepper	salt and pepper
lettuce for serving	lettuce for serving
sliced gherkins to garnish	sliced gherkins to garnish

Skin and fillet the mackerel.

Mix together the apple, beetroot, potato and soured cream. Season to taste.

Spread the lettuce leaves on four individual serving plates, top with mackerel and salad and scatter slices of gherkin on top.

Serve straightaway.

Chicken and Avocado Salad

SERVES 4–6

METRIC/IMPERIAL	AMERICAN
450 g/1 lb spinach or 1 lettuce	1 lb spinach or 1 lettuce
350 g/12 oz cooked chicken	¾ lb cooked chicken
4 sticks celery, chopped	4 stalks celery, chopped
50 g/2 oz walnuts, chopped	½ cup walnuts, chopped
1 avocado, peeled and chopped	1 avocado, peeled and chopped
French dressing:	*French dressing:*
3 tablespoons olive oil	¼ cup olive oil
1 tablespoon wine vinegar	1 tablespoon wine vinegar
salt and pepper	salt and pepper
1 clove garlic, crushed	1 clove garlic, crushed
pinch of dry mustard	dash of dry mustard

Tear the spinach or lettuce into bite-sized pieces. Cut the chicken into 2·5-cm/1-inch pieces.

To make the French dressing, put all the ingredients in a screw-top jar and shake vigorously until well combined.

Put all the salad ingredients in a bowl. Prepare the avocado last so that it does not discolour. Pour over the dressing and toss lightly. Serve as soon as possible.

Remoulade of Celeriac

SERVES 4

This is lovely served as a vegetable on its own, or try it with 225 g/8 oz peeled prawns folded in.

METRIC/IMPERIAL	AMERICAN
450 g/1 lb celeriac	1 lb celery root
450 g/1 lb carrots	1 lb carrots
50 g/2 oz walnuts, chopped	½ cup walnuts, chopped
3 tablespoons natural yogurt	¼ cup plain yogurt
lettuce for serving	lettuce for serving
few walnuts to garnish	few walnuts to garnish
Remoulade mayonnaise:	*Remoulade mayonnaise:*
150 ml/¼ pint mayonnaise	⅔ cup mayonnaise
1 teaspoon prepared mustard	1 teaspoon prepared mustard
1 teaspoon finely chopped capers	1 teaspoon finely chopped capers
1 teaspoon finely chopped gherkin	1 teaspoon finely chopped gherkin
1 teaspoon finely chopped parsley	1 teaspoon finely chopped parsley
few drops of anchovy essence (optional)	few drops of anchovy extract (optional)

Mix all the ingredients for the remoulade mayonnaise together gently but thoroughly.

Grate the celeriac and carrot directly into the mayonnaise, add the walnuts and yogurt and mix well.

Arrange the lettuce leaves on individual serving plates and pile the salad on top. Garnish with the walnut halves and serve as soon as possible.

Family Puddings

If your family is like mine, a pudding is a must to finish a meal. I try to keep them as simple as possible and have now built up a selection that I know the family like and are economical and easy to make. Some vary quite considerably, according to the time of year and what is in season, others are all the year round favourites that can be made from storecupboard ingredients.

The summer desserts tend to be light and need the minimum of cooking – ice cream, jellies, fruit and so on. It is in the winter, when the family comes in cold and hungry, that a good old-fashioned hot family pudding is really appreciated. It should be quite filling but not stodgy; suet and sponge puddings, stewed fruit, milk or batter puddings, including fritters and pancakes are all good stand-bys that have so many flavours and variations you will not have to serve the same pudding twice for weeks at a time.

You will probably find old favourites in this selection of family puddings, others will be new to you. Do try them on your family, I am sure they will be appreciated.

Christmas Pudding

SERVES 6

A recipe to keep and use again and again, year after year. Serve with egg custard sauce (see right).

METRIC/IMPERIAL	AMERICAN
100 g/4 oz self-raising flour	1 cup all-purpose flour sifted with 1 teaspoon baking powder
100 g/4 oz fresh breadcrumbs	2 cups fresh soft bread crumbs
100 g/4 oz shredded suet	$\frac{2}{3}$ cup chopped suet
350 g/12 oz mixed dried fruit (apricots, raisins, sultanas, currants, dates, prunes)	2 cups mixed dried fruit (apricots, raisins, seedless white raisins, currants, dates, prunes)
50 g/2 oz mixed peel, chopped	$\frac{1}{3}$ cup chopped candied peel
50 g/2 oz almonds, chopped	$\frac{1}{2}$ cup almonds, chopped
100 g/4 oz dark soft brown sugar	$\frac{1}{2}$ cup dark soft brown sugar
grated rind and juice of 1 lemon	grated rind and juice of 1 lemon
grated rind and juice of 1 orange	grated rind and juice of 1 orange
$\frac{1}{2}$ teaspoon ground mixed spice	$\frac{1}{2}$ teaspoon ground mixed spice
$\frac{1}{4}$ teaspoon grated nutmeg	$\frac{1}{4}$ teaspoon grated nutmeg
pinch of salt	dash of salt
3 eggs, beaten	3 eggs, beaten
about 150 ml/$\frac{1}{4}$ pint dark brown ale or Guinness	about $\frac{2}{3}$ cup dark beer or Guinness

Put all the ingredients into a mixing bowl and mix thoroughly. It should be a soft dropping consistency – add a little more ale if necessary. Put the mixture into a greased 1·25-litre/2-pint (U.S. 2$\frac{1}{2}$-pint) pudding basin. Cover with a piece of greased foil and tie securely.

Put the basin in a saucepan with boiling water to come halfway up the side of the basin. Cover tightly and steam the pudding for 6 hours. Check the level of the water frequently and top up with more boiling water whenever necessary.

Either serve the pudding straightaway, or store in a cool place for up to 1 year.

To reheat, steam, as before, for a further 2 hours.

Egg Custard Sauce

MAKES 600 ml/1 pint (U.S. 2½ cups)

METRIC/IMPERIAL	AMERICAN
3 eggs	3 eggs
25 g/1 oz castor sugar	2 tablespoons sugar
600 ml/1 pint milk	2½ cups milk
few drops of vanilla essence or 1 tablespoon sherry	few drops of vanilla extract or 1 tablespoon sherry

Whisk the eggs and sugar together in a basin.

Heat the milk and vanilla essence until very warm but not boiling. Pour the milk on to the eggs, whisking well all the time.

Place the basin over a saucepan of gently simmering water and cook, stirring frequently, until the custard has thickened and will coat the back of the spoon.

Crusty Apple Charlotte

SERVES 4

METRIC/IMPERIAL	AMERICAN
3 slices white bread	3 slices white bread
75 g/3 oz demerara sugar	6 tablespoons light brown sugar
pinch each of ground cinnamon and cloves	dash each of ground cinnamon and cloves
450 g/1 lb cooking apples	1 lb baking apples
2 tablespoons golden syrup	3 tablespoons corn syrup
juice of 1 lemon	juice of 1 lemon

Remove the crusts from the bread and cut it into neat dice. Mix the sugar with the spices. Peel, core and slice the apples.

In a greased ovenproof dish, layer the apple, sugar and bread, making two layers of each and finishing with the bread dice. The dish should be piled high as the pudding settles down when cooked.

Heat the syrup and lemon juice together gently and drizzle over the bread. Bake in a moderate oven (180°C, 350°F, Gas Mark 4) for 1½ hours or until the apple is cooked and the bread crisp and golden. Serve hot.

Temperance Fruit Pie

SERVES 4

METRIC/IMPERIAL	AMERICAN
300 ml/½ pint stewed or canned fruit	1¼ cups stewed or canned fruit
1 (113-g/4-oz) carton cottage cheese	½ cup cottage cheese
1 tablespoon clear honey	1 tablespoon clear honey
150 g/5 oz desiccated coconut	1⅔ cups shredded coconut
25 g/1 oz plain wholemeal flour	¼ cup whole meal flour
25 g/1 oz soft brown sugar	2 tablespoons soft brown sugar
50 g/2 oz butter, melted	¼ cup melted butter

Put the fruit in an ovenproof dish, spread the cottage cheese over and drizzle the honey on top.

Mix together the coconut, flour, sugar and melted butter. Spread over the cottage cheese to cover it completely. Bake in a moderate oven (180°C, 350°F, Gas Mark 4) for 20 minutes or until hot and golden. Allow to stand for 5 minutes before serving.

Apricot Sour Crumble

SERVES 4

Try canned pineapple and peaches instead of apricots for a variation. Serve the juice separately in a jug.

METRIC/IMPERIAL	AMERICAN
1 (425-g/15-oz) can apricots	1 (15-oz) can apricots
1 (142-ml/5-fl oz) carton soured cream	1 (5-fl oz) carton dairy sour cream
1 egg	1 egg
75 g/3 oz soft brown sugar	6 tablespoons soft brown sugar
1 tablespoon plain flour	1 tablespoon all-purpose flour
few drops of vanilla essence	few drops of vanilla extract
Crumble:	*Crumble:*
50 g/2 oz plain wholemeal flour	½ cup whole meal flour
25 g/1 oz butter	2 tablespoons butter
25 g/1 oz demerera sugar	2 tablespoons light brown sugar
pinch of ground mixed spice	dash of ground mixed spice

Drain the apricots and spread them in an ovenproof pie dish.

Whip together the cream, egg, sugar, flour and essence. Spread the mixture over the apricots and bake in a moderate oven (180°C, 350°F, Gas Mark 4) for 15 minutes.

Meanwhile, put the flour for the crumble into a bowl. Add the butter and rub in until the mixture resembles breadcrumbs. Stir in the sugar and spice.

Spread the crumble over the soured cream mixture, return to the oven and bake for a further 20 minutes, or until golden and firm.

Serve hot.

Family Favourite Suet Pudding

SERVES 4

The cook's favourite because it is so easy and economical to make – one of the variations will surely be your family's favourite.

METRIC/IMPERIAL	AMERICAN
100 g/4 oz plain flour	1 cup all-purpose flour
2 teaspoons baking powder	2 teaspoons baking powder
100 g/4 oz shredded suet	⅔ cup chopped suet
100 g/4 oz fresh breadcrumbs	2 cups fresh soft bread crumbs
pinch of salt	dash of salt
100 g/4 oz castor sugar	½ cup sugar
1 egg, beaten	1 egg, beaten
about 150 ml/¼ pint milk	about ⅔ cup milk
sauce or flavouring of your choice (see opposite)	sauce or flavoring of your choice (see opposite)

Sift the flour and baking powder into a mixing bowl. Stir in all the remaining ingredients to make a soft dropping consistency and spoon into a greased 1·25-litre/2-pint (U.S. 2½-pint) basin.

Cover the basin with a double thickness of greased greaseproof paper or foil and secure with string. Put the basin in a saucepan with boiling water to come halfway up the sides. Cover the pan and steam for 2–2½ hours, topping up with boiling water as necessary. Turn the pudding out of the basin and serve.

Variations

Butter and sugar pudding Serve the plain pudding sprinkled with demerara sugar and a knob of butter.

Jam or marmalade pudding Put 3 or 4 tablespoons jam or marmalade in the bottom of the pudding basin before putting in the pudding. Serve with more jam.

Spicy syrup or treacle pudding Sift 1 teaspoon ground ginger or ground mixed spice with the flour when making the pudding. Put 3 – 4 tablespoons syrup or treacle in the bottom of the pudding basin before putting in the pudding. Serve with more syrup.

Apricot pudding Put 3 or 4 tablespoons orange marmalade or apricot jam in the pudding basin before putting in the pudding. Add 50 g/2 oz (U.S. $\frac{1}{3}$ cup) chopped dried apricot to the dry ingredients. Serve with more marmalade or jam.

College pudding Add 100 g/4 oz (U.S. $\frac{2}{3}$ cup) mixed dried fruit and $\frac{1}{2}$ teaspoon ground mixed spice to the dry ingredients. Serve with custard.

Chocolate pudding Blend 2 tablespoons (U.S. 3 tablespoons) cocoa with 2 tablespoons (U.S. 3 tablespoons) milk and stir into the pudding mixture with the milk. Serve with custard or chocolate sauce (see page 147).

Apple Sultana Pudding

SERVES 6

In the autumn use blackberries instead of sultanas.

METRIC/IMPERIAL	AMERICAN
Suetcrust pastry:	*Suet crust dough:*
225 g/8 oz self-raising flour	2 cups all-purpose flour sifted with 2 teaspoons baking powder
pinch of salt	dash of salt
100 g/4 oz shredded suet	⅔ cup chopped suet
cold water to mix	cold water to mix
Filling:	*Filling:*
450 g/1 lb cooking apples, peeled, cored and sliced	1 lb baking apples, peeled, cored and sliced
juice of 1 lemon	juice of 1 lemon
50 g/2 oz sultanas	⅓ cup seedless white raisins
1 teaspoon ground cinnamon	1 teaspoon ground cinnamon
75 g/3 oz demerera sugar	6 tablespoons light brown sugar

First make the pastry. Sift the flour and salt into a bowl. Stir in the suet then, mixing with a fork, add enough cold water to make a soft dough. Knead the pastry on a lightly floured surface. Roll out the pastry to a round large enough to line a 1·25-litre/2-pint (U.S. 2½-pint) pudding basin plus 2·5 cm/1 inch all round. Cut out a one-quarter section from the pastry and put aside to form a lid later. Damp the cut edges of the pastry then fit into the pudding basin to form an even lining. Press the edges together firmly. The pastry will stick up 1 cm/½ inch all around the basin – fold this inwards.

Mix the filling ingredients together and pile in to the lined basin. Roll out the reserved pastry to a round for the lid. Damp the edges of the pastry and place the lid in position. Press on firmly.

Cover the pudding basin with a double thickness of greased foil with a pleat across the centre. Tie firmly round the basin. Place the basin in a saucepan of boiling water so that the water comes halfway up the sides. Cover the saucepan and cook steadily for 2 hours. Check that the saucepan does not boil dry. Top up occasionally with more boiling water.

Caramel Vienna Pudding

SERVES 4

Serve with egg custard sauce (see page 93).

METRIC/IMPERIAL	AMERICAN
25 g/1 oz granulated sugar	2 tablespoons sugar
300 ml/½ pint milk	1¼ cups milk
4 thick slices white bread, crusts removed	4 thick slices white bread, crusts removed
2 eggs	2 eggs
few drops of vanilla essence or 1 tablespoon sherry	few drops of vanilla extract or 1 tablespoon sherry
50 g/2 oz sultanas	⅓ cup seedless white raisins
25 g/1 oz chopped mixed peel	3 tablespoons chopped candied peel
25 g/1 oz soft brown sugar	2 tablespoons soft brown sugar
finely grated rind of 1 lemon	finely grated rind of 1 lemon

Put the sugar in a saucepan with 4 tablespoons (U.S. ⅓ cup) water. Heat gently, stirring occasionally, until the sugar is dissolved. Cook until the sugar caramelises and is golden brown.

Remove the pan from the heat and add the milk. Stir, heating gently, until the caramel is dissolved.

Dice the bread. Beat the eggs and vanilla essence or sherry into the caramel milk. Strain on to the bread then stir in the remaining ingredients. Put aside for 30 minutes.

Put into a greased 600-ml/1-pint (U.S. 1½-pint) pudding basin and cover with foil. Put in a water bath with 2·5 cm/1 inch warm water.

Bake in a moderate oven (160°C, 325°F, Gas Mark 3) for 1½ hours, or until firm.

Turn the pudding out of the basin and serve as soon as possible.

Coconut Pudding

SERVES 6

Serve with marshmallow sauce (see below), custard or golden syrup.

METRIC/IMPERIAL	AMERICAN
150 ml/¼ pint evaporated milk	⅔ cup evaporated milk
50 g/2 oz desiccated coconut	⅔ cup shredded coconut
100 g/4 oz castor sugar	½ cup sugar
100 g/4 oz softened margarine	½ cup softened margarine
2 eggs, beaten	2 eggs, beaten
175 g/6 oz self-raising flour	1½ cups all-purpose flour sifted with 2 teaspoons baking powder
1 teaspoon baking powder	

Stir the evaporated milk and coconut together and leave for about 10 minutes to soak.

Put the sugar, margarine and eggs into a bowl. Sift in the flour and baking powder. Beat together for 2–3 minutes or until well mixed. Beat in the coconut mixture.

Put into a 1·25-litre/2-pint (U.S. 2½-pint) greased pudding basin and cover with greased foil. Put the basin in a saucepan with boiling water to come halfway up the sides. Cover the pan and steam for 2–2½ hours. Turn the pudding out of the basin and serve.

Marshmallow Sauce

My children's favourite substitute for custard.

METRIC/IMPERIAL	AMERICAN
75 g/3 oz marshmallows	3 oz marshmallows
150 ml/¼ pint evaporated milk	⅔ cup evaporated milk
few drops of vanilla essence	few drops of vanilla extract

Snip the marshmallows into quarters with scissors. Put all the ingredients in a basin and stand it over a saucepan of simmering water. Cook until warm and the marshmallows are almost dissolved. Serve at once.

Marmalade Bread and Butter Pudding

SERVES 4

METRIC/IMPERIAL	AMERICAN
6 thin slices bread, buttered	6 thin slices bread, buttered
3 tablespoons orange marmalade	¼ cup orange marmalade
50 g/2 oz mixed dried fruit	⅓ cup mixed dried fruit
25 g/1 oz soft brown sugar	2 tablespoons soft brown sugar
2 eggs	2 eggs
600 ml/1 pint milk	2½ cups milk
grated nutmeg for sprinkling	grated nutmeg for sprinkling

Make the bread and butter into sandwiches with the marmalade, but put the butter side outside. Remove the crusts and cut the sandwiches into quarters.

Put half the sandwiches in a greased 1·25-litre/2-pint (U.S. 2½-pint) ovenproof dish. Sprinkle with the fruit and half the sugar. Cover with the remaining sandwiches and sprinkle with the remaining sugar.

Beat the eggs and milk together then pour over the bread. Leave for 30 minutes.

Sprinkle the top with grated nutmeg and bake in a moderate oven (160°C, 325°F, Gas Mark 3) for 45 minutes, or until the pudding is set and crisp on top.

Black-eyed Apples

SERVES 4

METRIC/IMPERIAL	AMERICAN
8 prunes	8 prunes
150 ml/¼ pint apple juice	⅔ cup apple juice
50 g/2 oz soft brown sugar	¼ cup soft brown sugar
25 g/1 oz butter	2 tablespoons butter
¼ teaspoon ground cinnamon	¼ teaspoon ground cinnamon
4 large cooking apples	4 large baking apples

Soak the prunes in the apple juice overnight or simmer for 40 minutes until tender. Reserve the apple juice and stone the prunes. Beat the sugar, butter and cinnamon together.

Wash and core the apples. Score the skin round the circumference. Push a prune into the bottom of each then stuff with a quarter of the cinnamon mixture. Top with a prune.

Stand in an ovenproof dish and pour over the reserved apple juice. Bake in a moderate oven (180°C, 350°F, Gas Mark 4) for 30 minutes or until the apples are tender.

Serve as soon as possible.

Pancakes

SERVES 4

Pancakes are a good economical family dessert. They can be made just before they are eaten or ahead of time if preferred. They can be served in a wide variety of ways.

METRIC/IMPERIAL	AMERICAN
Batter:	*Batter:*
100 g/4 oz plain flour	1 cup all-purpose flour
1 egg	1 egg
1 egg yolk	1 egg yolk
300 ml/½ pint water	1¼ cups water
lard for frying	shortening for frying
filling (see below)	filling (see below)

Sift the flour into a mixing bowl. Stir in the egg and egg yolk with half the water. Beat to a smooth batter then stir in the remaining water.

Use a small heavy frying pan (15-cm/6-inch diameter is ideal). Heat a small knob of lard in it so that the base is just greased.

Pour enough batter in the pan to make a thin layer. Tilt the pan to allow the batter to spread. Cook quickly until lightly browned underneath then flip or toss over and cook the other side.

Place the cooked pancake on a plate and either allow to cool or place the plate over a saucepan of hot water to keep hot. Stack subsequent pancakes one on top of the other as they are made.

Using a 15-cm/6-inch pan, this amount of batter should make 12 thin pancakes – three per person.

Fruit Custard Pancakes

SERVES 4

METRIC/IMPERIAL	AMERICAN
1 quantity pancakes (see opposite)	1 quantity pancakes (see opposite)
Filling:	*Filling:*
1 (425-g/15-oz) can fruit (pineapple, mandarins, peaches or apricots)	1 (15-oz) can fruit (pineapple, tangerines, peaches or apricots)
2 egg yolks	2 egg yolks
50 g/2 oz castor sugar	$\frac{1}{4}$ cup sugar
1 tablespoon cornflour	1 tablespoon cornstarch
finely grated rind of 1 lemon	finely grated rind of 1 lemon
150 ml/$\frac{1}{4}$ pint milk	$\frac{2}{3}$ cup milk

Make the pancakes and keep hot (see opposite).

Drain the fruit and reserve the syrup. Whisk the egg yolks with the sugar, cornflour, lemon rind and milk until smooth. Put in a saucepan and cook gently, stirring, until thickened and smooth. Stir in the drained fruit.

Divide the filling between the pancakes and roll up. Put in a shallow ovenproof dish in a single layer and reheat, if necessary, in a moderate oven (180°C, 350°F, Gas Mark 4) for 10–15 minutes.

Heat the reserved fruit syrup and serve with the pancakes.

Spicy Fritters

SERVES 4

METRIC/IMPERIAL	AMERICAN
175 g/6 oz plain flour	1½ cups all-purpose flour
1 teaspoon ground cinnamon	1 teaspoon ground cinnamon
1½ teaspoons baking powder	1¼ teaspoons baking powder
pinch of salt	dash of salt
1 egg	1 egg
150 ml/¼ pint milk	⅔ cup milk
few drops of vanilla essence	few drops of vanilla extract
oil for deep frying	oil for deep frying
castor sugar for sprinkling	superfine sugar for sprinkling
Orange Sauce (see below) for serving	Orange Sauce (see below) for serving

Sift the flour, cinnamon, baking powder and salt into a mixing bowl. Add the egg, milk and vanilla essence, beating well all the time to make a smooth batter.

Heat the oil for deep frying (see Fruit Fritters, right) and fry teaspoons of the batter until golden. Drain well on absorbent kitchen paper.

Serve as soon as possible, sprinkled with castor sugar. Hand the orange sauce separately.

Orange Sauce

MAKES ABOUT 300 ml/½ pint

METRIC/IMPERIAL	AMERICAN
300 ml/½ pint orange juice	1¼ cups orange juice
finely grated rind and juice of 1 lemon	finely grated rind and juice of 1 lemon
15 g/½ oz cornflour	2 tablespoons cornstarch
1 tablespoon honey	1 tablespoon honey

Put all the ingredients in a small saucepan and bring to the boil, stirring all the time. Boil for 1–2 minutes. Serve as soon as possible.

Fruit Fritters

SERVES 4

Serve with custard, cream or orange sauce. Egg Custard Sauce (see page 93) is also good.

METRIC/IMPERIAL	AMERICAN
450 g/1 lb apples or 8 pineapple rings or 4 bananas	1 lb apples or 8 pineapple rings or 4 bananas
oil for deep frying	oil for deep frying
castor sugar for sprinkling	superfine sugar for sprinkling
Batter:	*Batter:*
100 g/4 oz plain flour	1 cup all-purpose flour
1 tablespoon castor sugar	1 tablespoon sugar
pinch of grated nutmeg or ground mixed spice	dash of grated nutmeg or ground mixed spice
150 ml/¼ pint water	⅔ cup water
1 tablespoon oil	1 tablespoon oil
1 egg white	1 egg white

First prepare the fruit; peel and core apples and cut into 1-cm/½-inch thick rings and leave in salted water until needed; drain pineapple rings very well; peel bananas and cut each into three chunks.

To make the batter, sift the flour into a bowl. Add the sugar and spice. Whisk in half the water, beating to make a smooth batter. Stir in the remaining water and oil.

Just before needed, whisk the egg white until stiff and fold in.

Fill a deep frying pan a half to one-third full of oil and heat to 190°C/375°F (a 1-cm/½-inch cube of bread will brown in about 30 seconds).

Make sure the fruit is as dry as possible then dip into the batter. Put the pieces straight into the hot oil, one at a time or they will stick together. Do not use a frying basket. Fry until light golden brown. Drain very well on absorbent kitchen paper. Serve as soon as possible, sprinkled with extra castor sugar.

Fruit Compote

SERVES 4 – 6

Stewed fruit with a difference. For special occasions, use wine instead of orange juice. Serve with custard or cream.

METRIC/IMPERIAL	AMERICAN
675 – 900 g/1½ – 2 lb fresh fruit (rhubarb, apples, gooseberries, plums, etc.)	1½ – 2 lb fresh fruit (rhubarb, apples, gooseberries, plums, etc.)
150 ml/¼ pint orange juice	⅔ cup orange juice
150 ml/¼ pint water	⅔ cup water
2 tablespoons honey or to taste	3 tablespoons honey or to taste
4 cloves	4 cloves
2·5-cm/1-inch piece cinnamon stick	1-inch piece cinnamon stick

Peel, core, slice, stone or otherwise prepare and clean the fruit, as necessary.

Put the orange juice, water and honey into a saucepan with the cloves and cinnamon. Bring to the boil, stirring. Add the fruit and simmer gently, covered, until just tender, but not mushy. The time will depend on the fruit.

Serve hot or chill in the syrup, and serve cold.

Apple and Orange Fool

SERVES 4 – 6

Rhubarb makes a good variation to use instead of apples. Chill the evaporated milk in the refrigerator overnight before using.

METRIC/IMPERIAL	AMERICAN
450 g/1 lb cooking apples	1 lb baking apples
grated rind and juice of 1 orange	grated rind and juice of 1 orange
100 g/4 oz castor sugar	½ cup sugar
4 eggs, beaten	4 eggs, beaten
150 ml/¼ pint evaporated milk, well chilled	⅔ cup evaporated milk, well chilled

Peel, core and thinly slice the apples.

Put in a saucepan with the orange rind and juice. Sprinkle with sugar, cover and cook very gently, stirring frequently, until soft and pulpy.

Blend the apple to a smooth purée in an electric blender.

Put the apple in a basin and beat in the eggs. Cook over a saucepan of simmering water, stirring frequently, until smooth and thick. Cool.

Whisk the evaporated milk until thick. Fold into the cold apple mixture and serve in individual dishes.

Peaches and Honey Fluff

SERVES 6–8

METRIC/IMPERIAL
2 (14-g/½-oz) envelopes
  powdered gelatine
1 (425-g/15-oz) can peach
  slices
150 ml/¼ pint clear honey
150 ml/¼ pint lemon juice
½ teaspoon ground ginger
  (optional)
150 ml/¼ pint evaporated
  milk, well chilled

AMERICAN
4 (7-g/¼-oz) envelopes
  gelatin
1 (15-oz) can peach slices
⅔ cup clear honey
⅔ cup lemon juice
½ teaspoon ground ginger
  (optional)
⅔ cup evaporated milk,
  well chilled

Put the gelatine in a small basin. Drain the peach slices, measure the syrup and make up to 600 ml/1 pint (U.S. 2½ cups) with water. Add half of this to the gelatine and mix well. Stand in a saucepan with water to come halfway up the sides of the basin. Heat, stirring occasionally, until the gelatine is dissolved.

Mix the remaining syrup and water with the honey, lemon juice and ginger and mix with the gelatine mixture when dissolved. Chill until syrupy.

Whisk the evaporated milk until thick and creamy. Fold in the gelatine mixture. Chop the peach slices, reserving some for decoration, and fold in. Pour into a 1·25-litre/2-pint (U.S. 2½-pint) mould and chill.

Unmould on to a serving plate and decorate with the reserved peach slices.

Mandarin Mist

SERVES 4

METRIC/IMPERIAL	AMERICAN
1 packet orange blancmange powder to make 600 ml/1 pint	1 package instant orange pudding powder to make 2½ cups
25 g/1 oz sugar	2 tablespoons sugar
450 ml/¾ pint milk	2 cups milk
1 (298-g/10½-oz) can mandarins	1 (10½-oz) can tangerines
1 egg white	1 egg white

Mix the blancmange with the sugar and a little of the milk. Boil the remaining milk and pour on to the mixture, stirring all the time. Return the mixture to the saucepan and boil for 1 minute, stirring continuously.

Drain the oranges, measure 150 ml/¼ pint (U.S. ⅔ cup) of the syrup and stir in with most of the mandarin segments, reserving some for decoration.

Whisk the egg white until stiff and fold in. Pile into four individual serving dishes and decorate with the remaining mandarins. Chill before serving.

Orange Water Ice

SERVES 6−8

METRIC/IMPERIAL	AMERICAN
1 orange	1 orange
1 lemon	1 lemon
900 ml/1½ pints water	3¾ cups water
225 g/8 oz granulated sugar	1 cup sugar
1 (14-g/½-oz) envelope powdered gelatine	2 (7-g/¼-oz) envelopes gelatin
1 (177-g/6¼-oz) can concentrated frozen orange juice, thawed	1 (6¼-oz) can concentrated frozen orange juice, thawed
1 egg white	1 egg white

Thinly peel the zest from the orange and lemon and put into a saucepan with the water and sugar. Bring to the boil, stirring until the sugar is dissolved. Boil rapidly for 5 minutes.

Dissolve the gelatine in a little hot (not boiling) syrup. Squeeze the orange and lemon juice. Add the gelatine, juice and concentrated orange to the syrup then strain into a shallow container. Cool and when cold, freeze until firm round the edges and mushy.

Whisk the egg white until stiff and fold in. Freeze again. If there is time, whisk again when half frozen.

School Holiday Ice Cream

SERVES 6−8

Homemade ice cream is much nicer than the shop-bought variety. The only difficulty is keeping up with demand. Try making two or three times this quantity at a time.

METRIC/IMPERIAL	AMERICAN
4 eggs, separated	4 eggs, separated
100 g/4 oz icing sugar	scant 1 cup sifted confectioner's sugar
300 ml/½ pint single cream	1¼ cups light cream
25 g/1 oz butter, melted	2 tablespoons butter, melted
few drops of vanilla essence	few drops of vanilla extract

Whisk the egg whites until stiff and standing in peaks. Sift the icing sugar and gradually whisk it into the egg white until the mixture is stiff and creamy. Stir in the egg yolks, cream, butter and vanilla. Pour into a shallow container and freeze without stirring for about 3 hours, or until firm.

Variation

Fruit ice cream Stir in 300 ml/½ pint (U.S. 1¼ cups) sieved thick fruit purée with the cream.

Desserts for Entertaining

When you entertain is the time to make those gorgeous desserts that take a little extra time to prepare. They need not be expensive but will probably be more exotic than you would normally serve to the family.

When you plan your menu, choose a dessert which will complement the rest of the meal. Choose a dessert that looks attractive and needs just the minimum of decoration at the last minute.

Desserts that are made with gelatine such as jellies and creams can be set in beautifully shaped moulds and look very elegant. For children, choose an animal mould–they are normally made of plastic and not expensive to buy. Sundae or parfait glasses or decorative glass serving dishes are all attractive ways of serving cold desserts; once you have them they can be used again and again for all kinds of desserts.

For a very inexpensive and impressive way of serving, try using the hollowed out peel of fruit. Oranges, grapefruit and lemons for small dishes; pineapple and melon for larger "bowls".

Keep a stock of those small finishing touches in your cupboard, chocolate vermicelli, flaked almonds, crystallised orange and lemon slices, crystallised violets, angelica, glacé cherries and so on. For very special occasions try frosting fruit–grapes, cherries, strawberries, mandarin orange segments, sprays of redcurrants or even mint leaves. Lightly whisk an egg white until just frothy; dip the cleaned fruit in the egg white and then into castor sugar. Leave until dry.

Ice Box Gâteaux

Ice box gâteaux are no-bake cakes which are sticky and luscious enough to make a super dessert when you entertain. They are all made on the same principle, layering biscuits or sponge with a delicious filling then chilling well before serving.

Lemon Delicious Ice Box Gâteau

SERVES 6 – 8

METRIC/IMPERIAL	AMERICAN
100 g/4 oz butter	$\frac{1}{2}$ cup butter
150 g/5 oz castor sugar	$\frac{3}{4}$ cup sugar
grated rind and juice of 2 lemons	grated rind and juice of 2 lemons
3 eggs, separated	3 eggs, separated
1 packet trifle sponges, halved	1 package trifle sponges, halved
For decoration:	For decoration:
whipped cream	whipped cream
crystallised lemon slices	candied lemon slices

Put the butter and sugar in a basin and cream them together until light and fluffy. Beat in the lemon rind and juice then the egg yolks. Stand the basin over a saucepan of hot water and cook until smooth and beginning to thicken. Whisk the egg whites until stiff and fold in.

Put a layer of trifle sponge halves in the base of a 1-kg/2-lb loaf tin and cover with half the lemon mixture. Add another layer of sponges, the remaining lemon mixture then the remaining sponges. Press down lightly then chill for at least 3 hours, or until needed.

Unmould on to a plate then decorate with whipped cream and crystallised lemon slices.

Chocolate Brandy Ice Box Gâteau

SERVES 6 – 8

METRIC/IMPERIAL	AMERICAN
225 g/8 oz plain chocolate	$1\frac{1}{2}$ cups chocolate pieces
1 tablespoon coffee powder	1 tablespoon coffee powder
2 egg yolks	2 egg yolks
50 g/2 oz castor sugar	$\frac{1}{4}$ cup sugar
1 teaspoon vanilla essence	1 teaspoon vanilla extract
4 egg whites	4 egg whites
1 packet sponge fingers	1 package ladyfingers
1 tablespoon brandy	1 tablespoon brandy
For decoration:	For decoration:
whipped cream	whipped cream
grated chocolate	grated chocolate

Break the chocolate into pieces and put it in a basin. Stand the basin over a saucepan of hot water and leave until the chocolate has melted. Add the coffee, egg yolks, sugar and vanilla. Cook for a further 5 minutes, stirring occasionally, or until smooth and slightly thickened. Whisk the egg whites until stiff and fold in.

Layer the filling and sponge fingers in a 1-kg/2-lb loaf tin as for Lemon Delicious Ice Box Gâteau (see opposite). Sprinkle the sponge fingers with the brandy as you go. Chill.

To serve, unmould on to a plate, decorate the top with whipped cream and sprinkle with grated chocolate.

Jamaican Ice Box Gâteau

SERVES 6 – 8

METRIC/IMPERIAL	AMERICAN
100 g/4 oz butter	$\frac{1}{2}$ cup butter
100 g/4 oz soft brown sugar	$\frac{1}{2}$ cup soft brown sugar
2 egg yolks	2 egg yolks
2 tablespoons coffee essence	3 tablespoons coffee extract
2 bananas	2 bananas
1 tablespoon rum	1 tablespoon rum
4 tablespoons double cream	$\frac{1}{3}$ cup heavy cream
1 packet sponge fingers	1 package ladyfingers
For decoration:	*For decoration:*
whipped cream	whipped cream
banana	banana

Put the butter and sugar in a basin and cream them together until light and fluffy. Beat in the egg yolks and coffee essence. Stand the bowl over a saucepan of hot water and cook until smooth and beginning to thicken. Purée the bananas with the rum in an electric blender. Whip the cream until stiff. Stir the bananas and cream into the coffee mixture.

Layer the filling and sponge fingers in a 1-kg/2-lb loaf tin as for Lemon Delicious Ice Box Gâteau (see opposite).

Unmould on to a plate then decorate with whipped cream. Arrange thin slices of banana on top. Serve straightaway.

Grapefruit Cheesecake

SERVES 8–10

In the soft fruit season, try serving this cheesecake with fresh raspberries or strawberries.

METRIC/IMPERIAL	AMERICAN
Crumbcrust:	*Crumbcrust:*
225 g/8 oz digestive biscuits, crushed	3 cups graham cracker crumbs
½ teaspoon grated nutmeg	½ teaspoon grated nutmeg
½ teaspoon ground cinnamon	½ teaspoon ground cinnamon
pinch of ground cloves	dash of ground cloves
75 g/3 oz butter, melted	6 tablespoons butter, melted
Filling:	*Filling:*
2 grapefruit	2 grapefruit
2 eggs	2 eggs
175 g/6 oz castor sugar	⅔ cup sugar
1 (14-g/½-oz) envelope powdered gelatine	2 (7-g/¼-oz) envelopes gelatin
grated rind and juice of 1 lemon	grated rind and juice of 1 lemon
350 g/12 oz cream or curd cheese	¾ lb cream or curd cheese
450 ml/¾ pint whipping cream	2 cups whipping cream

Mix the biscuit crumbs with all the remaining crumbcrust ingredients. Press the mixture over the base of a 23-cm/9-inch springform or deep loose-bottomed cake tin. Chill.

Make the filling. Grate the rind finely from one of the grapefruit. Peel the skin and pith from both grapefruit then cut into segments (do this over a plate to collect the juice). Reserve eight segments and chop the remainder coarsely. Reserve the juice and make up to 150 ml/¼ pint (U.S. ⅔ cup) with water if necessary. Put 1 egg and 1 egg yolk in a bowl with the sugar. Whisk until thick, creamy and light in colour. Put 3 tablespoons (U.S.¼ cup) grapefruit juice in a small basin and add the gelatine. Stand in a saucepan of hot water, stirring occasionally until the gelatine is dissolved, then mix into the egg mixture with the grapefruit juice and rind, lemon juice and rind, chopped grapefruit segments and cream cheese. Whip the cream and stir in two-thirds. Whisk the remaining egg white until stiff and fold into the mixture.

Pour into the chilled crumbcrust and chill until firm. Remove from the tin. Decorate with piped rosettes of the remaining cream and the reserved grapefruit segments.

Baked Chocolate Almond Cheesecake

SERVES 6

METRIC/IMPERIAL	AMERICAN
Crumbcrust:	*Crumbcrust:*
225 g/8 oz digestive biscuits, crushed	3 cups graham cracker crumbs
75 g/3 oz butter, melted	6 tablespoons butter, melted
Filling:	*Filling:*
2 eggs, separated	2 eggs, separated
75 g/3 oz castor sugar	6 tablespoons sugar
225 g/8 oz cream or curd cheese	½ lb cream or curd cheese
25 g/1 oz ground almonds	¼ cup ground almonds
150 ml/¼ pint whipping cream	⅔ cup whipping cream
25 g/1 oz cocoa powder	¼ cup cocoa powder
2 teaspoons rum (optional)	2 teaspoons rum (optional)
icing sugar for decoration	confectioner's sugar for decoration

First prepare the crumbcrust. Mix the ingredients together and press over the base and up the sides of a deep 20-cm/8-inch round cake tin.

To make the filling, whisk the egg yolks and sugar together until light and fluffy. Beat in the cream cheese and ground almonds with the cream and cocoa. Add the rum if used. Whisk the egg whites until stiff and fold in. Put the filling into the crumbcrust and bake in a moderate oven (160°C, 325°F, Gas Mark 3) for 30–40 minutes, or until firm. Serve hot, dusted with icing sugar.

Redcurrants with Cream Cheese

SERVES 6

METRIC/IMPERIAL	AMERICAN
450 g/1 lb cream cheese	1 lb cream cheese
150 ml/¼ pint whipping cream	⅔ cup whipping cream
100 g/4 oz castor sugar	½ cup superfine sugar
225 g/8 oz redcurrant jelly	⅔ cup redcurrant jelly
350 g/12 oz redcurrants	¾ lb redcurrants

Put the cream cheese, cream and sugar in a bowl and beat well until thoroughly mixed. Line a sieve with muslin or a disposable kitchen cloth. Put in the cream cheese mixture and leave to drain for at least 8 hours.

Melt the redcurrant jelly very gently until warm, not hot. Remove from the heat and stir in the redcurrants.

Press the cream cheese mixture into six individual serving glasses. Spoon the redcurrant jelly over the top. Chill before serving.

Brandied Apricot Trifle

SERVES 6

METRIC/IMPERIAL	AMERICAN
1 packet trifle sponges	1 package trifle sponges
3 tablespoons apricot jam	¼ cup apricot jam
1 (425-g/15-oz) can apricots	1 (15-oz) can apricots
3 tablespoons brandy	¼ cup brandy
150 ml/¼ pint whipped cream	⅔ cup whipped cream
toasted flaked almonds for decoration	toasted flaked almonds for decoration
Custard:	*Custard:*
150 ml/¼ pint single cream	⅔ cup light cream
1 egg	1 egg
25 g/1 oz castor sugar	2 tablespoons sugar
few drops of vanilla essence	few drops of vanilla extract

Cut the sponges in half and spread with apricot jam. Drain the apricots, reserve six for decoration. Put the brandy in a measuring jug and make up to 150 ml/¼ pint (U.S. ⅔ cup) with apricot syrup.

Next prepare the custard. Mix all the ingredients in a basin and stand it over a saucepan of gently simmering water. Cook, stirring frequently, until thickened.

Arrange the sponges in one large or six individual serving dishes. Sprinkle with the brandy and syrup mixture and spread the apricots over the top. Pour over the hot custard. Leave until cold and firm.

Spread the cream over the top and decorate with toasted flaked almonds and the reserved apricots.

Barossa Cream

SERVES 6

METRIC/IMPERIAL	AMERICAN
100 g/4 oz dried apricots	¼ lb dried apricots
few drops of lemon juice	few drops of lemon juice
50 g/2 oz castor sugar	¼ cup sugar
¼ teaspoon vanilla essence	¼ teaspoon vanilla extract
150 ml/¼ pint whipping cream	⅔ cup whipping cream
50 g/2 oz flaked almonds, toasted	½ cup flaked almonds, toasted
Brandied grapes:	*Brandied grapes:*
100 g/4 oz seedless grapes	¼ lb seedless grapes
2 teaspoons brandy	2 teaspoons brandy

Cook the apricots with the lemon juice, sugar and the very minimum of water until very tender. Blend to a thick, smooth purée in an electric blender, or press through a sieve. Beat in the vanilla essence and cool. Whip the cream until stiff then fold into the apricot purée. Chill.

Make the brandied grapes. Cut the grapes in half and mix with the brandy. Chill.

Just before serving, put the apricot cream into a bowl, scatter with the almonds and pile the brandied grapes on top.

Chocolate Rum Pots

SERVES 6

A very rich chocolate mousse.

METRIC/IMPERIAL	AMERICAN
175 g/6 oz plain chocolate	1 cup dark chocolate pieces
3 eggs, separated	3 eggs, separated
1 tablespoon rum	1 tablespoon rum
15 g/½ oz butter	1 tablespoon butter
For decoration:	*For decoration:*
whipped cream	whipped cream
grated chocolate	grated chocolate

Break the chocolate into pieces and put into a basin. Stand the basin over a saucepan of hot water and leave until the chocolate is melted. Mix in the egg yolks, rum and butter and cook for 5 minutes, stirring occasionally.

Whisk the egg whites until stiff and fold into the chocolate mixture using a metal spoon. Divide between six individual pots or dishes. Chill until firm.

Decorate with a rosette of whipped cream and sprinkle with grated chocolate.

Frozen Apricot Mousse

SERVES 8

METRIC/IMPERIAL	AMERICAN
1 (822-g/1 lb 13-oz) can apricots	1 (29-oz) can apricots
4 tablespoons lemon juice	⅓ cup lemon juice
3 egg whites	3 egg whites
50 g/2 oz castor sugar	¼ cup sugar
150 ml/¼ pint whipping cream	⅔ cup whipping cream

Drain the apricots, chop half of them coarsely and reserve. Purée the remaining apricots in an electric blender with the lemon juice.

Whisk the egg whites until stiff then gradually whisk in the sugar. Whip the cream until thick.

Stir the cream and reserved apricots into the purée then gently fold in the egg whites with a metal spoon. Put in a plastic freezer container and freeze until set.

Spoon into individual bowls for serving.

Coffee Cream Cheese Mousse

SERVES 6–8

METRIC/IMPERIAL	AMERICAN
1 (14-g/½-oz) envelope powdered gelatine	2 (7-g/¼-oz) envelopes gelatin
450 g/1 lb cream cheese	1 lb cream cheese
6 eggs, separated	6 eggs, separated
100 g/4 oz castor sugar	½ cup sugar
1 tablespoon coffee essence	1 tablespoon coffee extract
For decoration:	*For decoration:*
whipped cream	whipped cream
hazelnuts or walnut halves	hazelnuts or walnut halves

Put the gelatine in a small basin with 3 tablespoons (U.S. ¼ cup) hot water. Place the cup in a saucepan of simmering water and leave, stirring occasionally until dissolved.

Put the cream cheese in a bowl. Beat in the egg yolks, sugar, coffee essence and gelatine. Leave in a cool place until beginning to set.

Whisk the egg whites until stiff and fold in. Pour into one large or six individual serving dishes and chill until set.

Serve decorated with rosettes of cream and hazelnuts or walnut halves.

Lemon Soufflé

SERVES 4

METRIC/IMPERIAL	AMERICAN
3 eggs, separated	3 eggs, separated
75 g/3 oz castor sugar	6 tablespoons sugar
grated rind and juice of 2 lemons	grated rind and juice of 2 lemons
1 (14-g/½-oz) envelope powdered gelatine	2 (7-g/¼-oz) envelopes gelatin
150 ml/¼ pint double cream	⅔ cup heavy cream
For decoration:	*For decoration:*
chopped nuts	chopped nuts
whipped cream	whipped cream

Lightly grease a 600-ml/1-pint (U.S. 1½-pint) capacity soufflé dish. Cut a double strip of greaseproof paper, the height of the dish plus 5 cm/2 inches and long enough to go right round the dish. Lightly grease the top 5 cm/2 inches of paper and tie it around the dish, greased side inside.

Place the egg yolks and sugar in a basin and whisk them together, over a saucepan of gently simmering water, until thick and creamy. Add the lemon rind and juice.

Put the gelatine in a small basin with 3 tablespoons (U.S. ¼ cup) water. Put the basin in a saucepan of hot water and leave until the gelatine is dissolved, stirring occasionally.

Whisk the egg whites until they stand in soft peaks. Whip the cream until thickened.

Stir the gelatine into the lemon mixture then fold in the cream and finally the egg. Turn into the prepared dish and leave in a cool place until set.

Before serving, carefully ease the greaseproof paper away from the soufflé using the back of a knife.

Press chopped nuts around the edges and decorate the top with rosettes of cream.

Variations

Orange soufflé Follow the recipe for Lemon Soufflé but use the grated rind and juice of 1 large orange plus 1 tablespoon lemon juice instead of the 2 lemons. For special occasions add 1 tablespoon Grand Marnier too and decorate with orange slices.

Chocolate Barbados soufflé Follow the recipe for Lemon Soufflé but use 75 g/3 oz chocolate (U.S. $\frac{1}{2}$ cup chocolate pieces) melted in 2 tablespoons (U.S. 3 tablespoons) milk instead of the 2 lemons. Add 1 tablespoon rum. Use toasted coconut to press round the outside instead of nuts.

Coffee soufflé Follow the recipe for Lemon Soufflé but use 150 ml/$\frac{1}{4}$ pint (U.S. $\frac{2}{3}$ cup) strong black coffee instead of the 2 lemons. For special occasions add 1 tablespoon Tia Maria too.

Pineapple Ginger Chantilly

SERVES 6–8

METRIC/IMPERIAL	AMERICAN
1 (376-g/13¼-oz) can crushed pineapple	1 (13¼-oz) can crushed pineapple
300 ml/½ pint double cream	1¼ cups heavy cream
25 g/1 oz icing sugar, sifted	¼ cup sifted confectioner's sugar
1 (227-g/8-oz) packet gingernuts	1 (8-oz) package gingersnaps
For decoration:	*For decoration:*
crystallised ginger (optional)	candied ginger (optional)
flaked almonds, toasted	flaked almonds, toasted

Drain the pineapple. Whip the cream until thick then fold in the pineapple pieces and icing sugar.

Sandwich the biscuits, one on top of the other, with half the cream. Carefully put the roll on its side and wrap in greaseproof paper or foil. Leave for at least 2–3 hours, overnight if necessary.

Just before serving, put the roll on a serving plate and cover with the remaining cream. Slice the crystallised ginger. Press the almonds over the roll and arrange the ginger on top.

Serve sliced obliquely. The biscuits make a decorative effect.

Syllabub

SERVES 10

METRIC/IMPERIAL	AMERICAN
2 lemons	2 lemons
150 ml/¼ pint white wine	⅔ cup white wine
3 tablespoons brandy	¼ cup brandy
100 g/4 oz castor sugar	½ cup sugar
450 ml/¾ pint double cream	2 cups heavy cream
sponge fingers for serving	ladyfingers for serving

Peel the lemon rind thinly with a vegetable peeler, taking only the zest – no pith. Squeeze out the lemon juice and put it in a bowl with the lemon rind, wine and brandy. Cover and put aside overnight.

Strain the wine mixture into a large bowl, then add the sugar and stir until dissolved. Stir in the cream. Whisk well until stiff and able to hold its shape. Pour into individual serving glasses and serve at once, with a sponge finger in each. If not served promptly, the syllabub will separate. It can be whisked up to its former stiffness again if this happens.

Soured Grapes Brulée

SERVES 4–6

METRIC/IMPERIAL	AMERICAN
450 g/1 lb seedless grapes	1 lb seedless grapes
2 (142-ml/5-fl oz) cartons soured cream	2 (5-fl oz) cartons dairy sour cream
100 g/4 oz soft brown sugar sugar	½ cup soft brown sugar

Place the grapes in a shallow flameproof dish. Spread the soured cream over the grapes and sprinkle with enough brown sugar to make a 3-mm/⅛-inch layer. Chill.

Cook under a hot grill until the sugar is melted. Serve at once, or cool then chill until needed.

Spiced Caramel Oranges

SERVES 4

METRIC/IMPERIAL	AMERICAN
4 large oranges	4 large oranges
50 g/2 oz dried apricots, chopped	⅓ cup dried apricots, chopped
275 g/10 oz granulated sugar	1¼ cups sugar
pinch of ground cinnamon	dash of ground cinnamon
pinch of ground cloves	dash of ground cloves

Peel the rind of two of the oranges very thinly with a vegetable peeler. Slice thinly into matchstick strips. Simmer the strips in a small saucepan with the apricots and enough water to cover for 10 minutes, or until the peel is very tender. Drain and put aside.

Peel all the pith and rind from all the oranges and slice into rounds. Do this over a plate to collect the juice.

Put the sugar in a saucepan with 150 ml/¼ pint (U.S. ⅔ cup) water, cinnamon and cloves. Bring to the boil, stirring all the time, then boil rapidly without stirring until the syrup is caramel coloured. Remove from the heat and add 3 tablespoons (U.S. ¼ cup) cold water and the collected orange juice. Return to the heat and stir until the caramel is dissolved.

Arrange the orange slices in a shallow serving dish and scatter the apricots and orange rind over the top.

Pour the caramel over the oranges and chill well before serving.

Mandarin Sweet and Sour

SERVES 6–8

METRIC/IMPERIAL	AMERICAN
2 (298-g/10½-oz) cans mandarins	2 (10½-oz) cans tangerines
1 (14-g/½-oz) envelope powdered gelatine	2 (7-g/¼-oz) envelopes gelatin
1 (142-ml/5-fl oz) carton soured cream	1 (5-fl oz) carton dairy sour cream
1 (142-ml/5-fl oz) carton natural yogurt	1 (5-fl oz) carton plain yogurt

Drain the mandarin oranges. Measure the syrup and make up to 300 ml/½ pint (U.S. 1¼ cups) with cold water. Reserve some segments for decoration and chop the remainder coarsely.

Put the gelatine in a small basin with half the measured syrup. Stand it in a saucepan with hot water to come halfway up the sides of the basin. Leave, stirring occasionally, until the gelatine is dissolved. Add the remaining syrup and leave in a cool place until just beginning to set. Fold in the chopped mandarins, soured cream and yogurt. Spoon into one large or several individual serving dishes and leave in a cool place until set.

Serve decorated with the reserved mandarin segments.

Caribbean Plum Pot

SERVES 3 – 4

METRIC/IMPERIAL	AMERICAN
450 g/1 lb plums	1 lb plums
50 g/2 oz soft brown sugar	$\frac{1}{4}$ cup soft brown sugar
2 tablespoons water	3 tablespoons water
2 tablespoons rum	3 tablespoons rum
2 tablespoons lime juice	3 tablespoons lime juice
pinch of ground cinnamon	dash of ground cinnamon
whipping cream for serving	whipping cream for serving

Wash the plums, cut in half and remove the stones. Put the sugar, water, rum, lime juice and cinnamon in a saucepan and bring to the boil, stirring until the sugar is dissolved. Add the plums and cook very gently for 20 minutes or until tender. Cool.

This dish can be served as it is or, more traditionally, it is puréed first to a thick fruit soup. Serve chilled with a little cream poured into the centre.

Strawberries in Raspberry Sauce

SERVES 4–6

METRIC/IMPERIAL	AMERICAN
450 g/1 lb strawberries	1 lb strawberries
225 g/8 oz raspberries	½ lb raspberries
3 tablespoons orange juice or 1 tablespoon Grand Marnier	¼ cup orange juice or 1 tablespoon Grand Marnier
icing sugar to taste	confectioner's sugar to taste
mint leaves for decoration (optional)	mint leaves for decoration (optional)

Clean and hull the strawberries, place in a serving bowl.
Purée the raspberries in an electric blender with the orange juice or Grand Marnier. Sieve the purée to remove the pips. Sweeten with icing sugar to taste. Chill well.

Just before serving, pour the sauce over the strawberries and decorate with mint leaves.

Italian Macaroon Peaches

SERVES 6

METRIC/IMPERIAL	AMERICAN
6 large peaches	6 large peaches
8 macaroon biscuits, crushed	8 macaroon cookies, crushed
1 tablespoon chopped mixed peel	1 tablespoon chopped candied peel
75 g/3 oz nibbed almonds	$\frac{3}{4}$ cup nibbed almonds
1 tablespoon Cointreau	1 tablespoon Cointreau
4 tablespoons white wine	$\frac{1}{3}$ cup white wine
25 g/1 oz castor sugar	2 tablespoons sugar

Cut the peaches in half and remove the stones. Scoop out about one-third of the flesh and chop finely.

Place the halves in an ovenproof dish. Mix the chopped peach with the crushed macaroons, mixed peel, almonds and Cointreau. Fill the peach halves with this mixture.

Spoon the wine over the top and sprinkle with the sugar. Bake in a moderate oven (180°C, 350°F, Gas Mark 4) for 20–25 minutes. Serve warm or cold.

Deep South Banana Split

SERVES 4

METRIC/IMPERIAL	AMERICAN
50 g/2 oz butter	$\frac{1}{4}$ cup butter
50 g/2 oz soft brown sugar	$\frac{1}{4}$ cup soft brown sugar
4 bananas	4 bananas
pinch of ground cinnamon	dash of ground cinnamon
2 tablespoons orange juice	3 tablespoons orange juice
1 tablespoon rum	1 tablespoon rum
4 scoops vanilla ice cream	4 scoops vanilla ice cream
slices of orange for decoration	slices of orange for decoration

Melt the butter and sugar together in a saucepan. Peel the bananas, cut in half lengthways and cook in the butter and sugar for 2–3 minutes.

Put the bananas on four serving dishes. Stir the cinnamon, orange juice and rum into the saucepan and heat. Place the scoops of ice cream on top of the bananas and spoon the cinnamon and rum sauce over.

Serve immediately, decorated with slices of orange.

Iced Raspberries with Melon

SERVES 4

METRIC/IMPERIAL	AMERICAN
225 g/8 oz raspberries	$\frac{1}{2}$ lb raspberries
2 small ogen melons	2 small ogen melons
2 tablespoons icing sugar, sifted	3 tablespoons confectioner's sugar, sifted
1 tablespoon brandy	1 tablespoon brandy
4 scoops raspberry ripple ice cream	4 scoops raspberry ripple ice cream

Hull the raspberries and chill well with the melon. Mix the raspberries with the icing sugar and brandy.

Cut the melons in half and scoop out the seeds. Put a scoop of ice cream in each and top with the raspberries. Serve immediately.

Ice Cream with Gooseberries

SERVES 4

METRIC/IMPERIAL	AMERICAN
450 g/1 lb gooseberries	1 lb gooseberries
2 tablespoons castor sugar	3 tablespoons sugar
2 heads elderflower (optional)	2 heads elderflower (optional)
150 ml/$\frac{1}{4}$ pint water	$\frac{2}{3}$ cup water
1 tablespoon cornflour	1 tablespoon cornstarch
juice of 2 oranges	juice of 2 oranges
8 scoops vanilla ice cream	8 scoops vanilla ice cream

Top and tail the gooseberries, rinse in cold water and drain well.

Put the sugar, elderflowers and water in a saucepan. Bring to the boil, stirring until the sugar is dissolved. Add the gooseberries and simmer for 15 minutes or until tender. Remove the elderflowers.

Mix the cornflour and orange juice together and stir into the gooseberries. Bring to the boil, stirring all the time. Simmer 1–2 minutes.

Just before serving, put the ice cream into four individual serving bowls and spoon the warm or cold gooseberry sauce over. Serve immediately.

Pastries and Pies

Most cooks love pastries and pies. They are a way to show your skill in cooking that is appreciated by everyone. Whether you are cooking for the family or entertaining, light crisp pastry is always enjoyed.

There are endless pastry dishes but they are nearly all made using basic pastry recipes.

Shortcrust pastry is the most versatile and possibly easiest to make and use. This chapter contains recipes for wholemeal, sweet, cheese and plain shortcrust. They are used for flans, large and small pies, and tartlets. It is possible to buy frozen shortcrust or packet mixes for shortcrust pastry but it is so easy to make yourself. Try making up your own mix – just rub the fat into the flour then store this in a screw-top jar in the refrigerator until needed. Weigh out as much or as little as you need for each recipe and mix to a dough with water.

Some recipes call for a ready-baked flan case which is baked blind. To bake blind, prepare the pastry according to the recipe and use to line a flan ring. Prick the base of the flan all over with a fork and line with a piece of greaseproof paper (a butter paper is ideal). Fill the flan with baking beans and cook the flan in a moderately hot oven (200°C, 400°F, Gas Mark 6) for about 15 minutes. Carefully remove the paper and beans and lift off the flan ring. Return to the oven and cook for a further 10 – 15 minutes.

Flaky and puff pastry are lovely to eat but, unfortunately, very time-consuming to make. The frozen and packet mixes are excellent however and, unless you have a lot of time to spare, worth using every time.

Choux pastry and hot water crust pastry are simple to make and very individual in their uses. Unlike other pastries, they like to be kept warm while being made. They are still quite easy to make but perhaps need a little practice. Choux pastry is an essential for éclairs, cream buns and profiteroles. Hot water crust is the traditional pastry for cold picnic pies such as pork pies.

Suet crust pastry is used in the chapter on Family Puddings when making an Apple Sultana Pudding. This could also have a savoury meat filling.

Shortcrust Pastry

MAKES 200 g/8 oz SHORTCRUST PASTRY

METRIC/IMPERIAL	AMERICAN
200 g/8 oz plain flour	2 cups all-purpose flour
pinch of salt	dash of salt
50 g/2 oz margarine	$\frac{1}{4}$ cup margarine
50 g/2 oz lard	$\frac{1}{4}$ cup shortening
about 2 tablespoons cold water	about 3 tablespoons cold water

Sift the flour and salt into a mixing bowl. Add the margarine and lard, cut into small pieces.

Rub the fat into the flour using your fingertips until the mixture resembles fine breadcrumbs.

Add the cold water and mix with a fork to make a crumbly dough. Add a little more water if necessary. Using your hand, knead the dough to make a firm ball.

Use as required.

Sweet Flan Pastry

Make as cheese pastry but omit the mustard and use 50 g/2 oz (U.S. $\frac{1}{4}$ cup) castor sugar in place of the cheese.

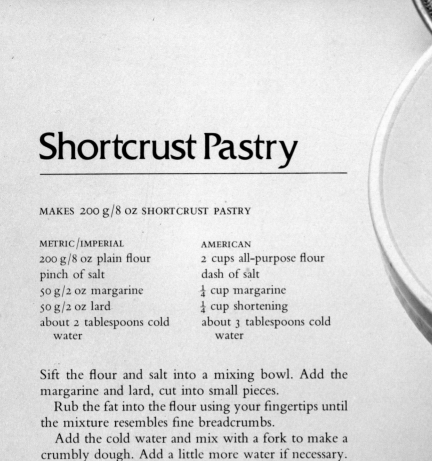

Cheese Pastry

MAKES 200 g/8 oz CHEESE PASTRY

This pastry can be used to make delicious cheese straws.

METRIC/IMPERIAL	AMERICAN
200 g/8 oz plain flour	2 cups all-purpose flour
pinch of salt	dash of salt
½ teaspoon dry mustard	½ teaspoon dry mustard
50 g/2 oz margarine	¼ cup margarine
50 g/2 oz lard	¼ cup shortening
100 g/4 oz dry Cheddar cheese, grated	1 cup grated dry Cheddar cheese
1 egg yolk	1 egg yolk
cold water to mix	cold water to mix

Sift together the flour, salt and mustard. Add the margarine and lard and rub in as for shortcrust pastry.

Stir in the cheese and egg yolk. Mixing with a fork, add enough cold water to make a firm dough. Chill and use as required.

Wholemeal Shortcrust Pastry

MAKES 200 g/8 oz WHOLEMEAL SHORTCRUST PASTRY

METRIC/IMPERIAL	AMERICAN
200 g/8 oz plain wholemeal flour	2 cups whole meal flour
pinch of salt	dash of salt
100 g/4 oz margarine or butter	½ cup margarine or butter
about 2 tablespoons cold water	about 3 tablespoons cold water

Mix the flour and salt together in a bowl then proceed as for shortcrust pastry.

Tomato Flan

SERVES 6

METRIC/IMPERIAL
175g/6oz Wholemeal
  Shortcrust Pastry (see
  page 133)
Filling:
1 tablespoon oil
1 onion, finely chopped
2 cloves garlic, crushed
1 (396-g/14-oz) can
  tomatoes
1 tablespoon tomato purée
4 tablespoons grated
  Parmesan cheese
pinch of dried oregano
salt and pepper
4 stuffed olives, sliced

AMERICAN
1½ cups Wholemeal
  Shortcrust Pastry (see
  page 133)
Filling:
1 tablespoon oil
1 onion, finely chopped
2 cloves garlic, crushed
1 (14-oz) can tomatoes
1 tablespoon tomato paste
⅓ cup grated Parmesan
  cheese
dash of dried oregano
salt and pepper
4 stuffed olives, sliced

Make the pastry and use to line a 20-cm/8-inch flan
ring. Bake blind (see page 130).

Heat the oil in a saucepan and fry the onion until
softened but not browned. Add the garlic, tomatoes,
tomato purée, all but 1 tablespoon of the Parmesan
cheese, oregano and seasoning. Bring to the boil and
simmer, uncovered, for 15 minutes, stirring frequently.

Spread the filling into the flan case and sprinkle with
the remaining Parmesan cheese and sliced olives. Bake
in a moderate oven (190°C, 375°F, Gas Mark 5) for 15
minutes or until the filling is firm.

Serve straight from the oven.

Mushroom Cheese Flan

SERVES 4

METRIC/IMPERIAL
175g/6oz Cheese Pastry
  (see page 133)
Filling:
25 g/1 oz butter
225 g/8 oz mushrooms,
  sliced
1 onion, chopped
150 ml/¼ pint milk
6 tablespoons cream
15 g/½ oz plain flour
2 egg yolks
salt and pepper
pinch of grated nutmeg
50 g/2 oz Cheddar cheese,
  grated
50 g/2 oz salami, thinly
  sliced

AMERICAN
1½ cups Cheese Pastry (see
  page 133)
Filling:
2 tablespoons butter
½ lb mushrooms, sliced
1 onion, chopped
⅔ cup milk
½ cup cream
2 tablespoons all-purpose
  flour
2 egg yolks
salt and pepper
dash of grated nutmeg
½ cup grated Cheddar
  cheese
2 oz salami, thinly sliced

Make the pastry and use to line a 20-cm/8-inch flan
ring. Bake blind (see page 130).

Heat the butter in a saucepan and fry the mushrooms
and onion until softened. Spread over the prepared flan
case. Add the milk, cream and flour to the saucepan and
bring to the boil, whisking all the time, until thickened
and smooth. Remove from the heat and whisk in the
egg yolks, seasoning and nutmeg. Pour into the flan
case and sprinkle the cheese on top.

Bake in a moderate oven (190°C, 375°F, Gas Mark 5)
for 15–20 minutes, or until the filling is firm. Arrange
the salami slices over the top and allow the flan to stand
for 5 minutes in a warm place before cutting.

Swiss Cheese Flan

SERVES 6

METRIC/IMPERIAL
175 g/6 oz Shortcrust
  Pastry (see page 132)
Filling:
350 g/12 oz streaky bacon,
  chopped
1 onion, chopped
100 /4 oz Gruyère cheese,
  grated
150 ml/¼ pint milk
6 tablespoons natural
  yogurt
25 g/1 oz plain flour
2 egg yolks
salt and pepper
pinch of grated nutmeg
1 egg white

AMERICAN
1½ cups Shortcrust Pastry
  (see page 132)
Filling:
¾ lb bacon slices, chopped
1 onion, chopped
1 cup grated Gruyère
  cheese
⅔ cup milk
½ cup plain yogurt
¼ cup all-purpose flour
2 egg yolks
salt and pepper
dash of grated nutmeg
1 egg white

Make the pastry and use to line a 20-cm/8-inch flan ring.

Fry the bacon in its own fat. Add the onion and cook until softened. Spread over the prepared flan case and spread the cheese on top.

Beat together the milk, yogurt, flour, egg yolks, seasoning and nutmeg. Whisk the egg white until stiff and fold into the mixture. Pour into the flan case and bake straightaway in a moderately hot oven (190°C, 375°F, Gas Mark 5) for 20 minutes. Reduce the temperature to moderate (180°C, 350°F, Gas Mark 4) and cook for a further 30–40 minutes, or until set. Serve straight from the oven.

Welsh Sausage Pie

SERVES 6

METRIC/IMPERIAL	AMERICAN
200 g/8 oz Shortcrust Pastry (see page 132)	½ lb Shortcrust Pastry see page 132)
beaten egg to glaze	beaten egg to glaze
Filling:	*Filling:*
50 g/2 oz butter	¼ cup butter
350 g/12 oz leeks, chopped	¾ lb leeks, chopped
225 g/8 oz pork sausagemeat	½ lb pork sausagemeat
½ teaspoon dried sage	½ teaspoon dried sage
salt and pepper	salt and pepper
50 g/2 oz Cheddar cheese, grated	½ cup grated Cheddar cheese
1 egg, beaten	1 egg, beaten
150 ml/¼ pint single cream	⅔ cup light cream

Roll out the pastry and use to line a 20-cm/8-inch shallow cake tin. Roll out a round for the lid at the same time.

Melt the butter in a frying pan and fry the leeks until softened, about 15 minutes. Remove the leeks and drain. Add the sausagemeat and fry until browned, stirring all the time. Drain off any excess fat. Mix in the leeks, sage and seasoning.

Spread half the cheese in the pastry case, cover with the sausage mixture then with the remaining cheese. Beat the egg with the cream and pour over.

Damp the pastry edges and cover with the pastry lid. Crimp the edges and glaze with beaten egg. Make a vent in the pastry lid and decorate with the pastry trimmings. Bake in a moderately hot oven (200°C, 400°F, Gas Mark 6) for 20–30 minutes, or until golden and cooked. Serve hot or cold.

Small Beef and Mushroom Pies

SERVES 6

METRIC/IMPERIAL	AMERICAN
350 g/12 oz Shortcrust Pastry (see page 132)	¾ lb Shortcrust Pastry (see page 132)
beaten egg to glaze	beaten egg to glaze
Filling:	*Filling:*
450 g/1 lb minced beef	1 lb ground beef
1 small onion, chopped	1 small onion, chopped
1 tablespoon oil	1 tablespoon oil
1 tablespoon plain flour	1 tablespoon all-purpose flour
150 ml/¼ pint beef stock or half stock and half red wine	⅔ cup beef stock or half stock and half red wine
1 clove garlic, crushed	1 clove garlic, crushed
100 g/4 oz mushrooms, sliced	¼ lb mushrooms, sliced
1 tablespoon orange juice	1 tablespoon orange juice
finely grated rind of 1 orange	finely grated rind of 1 orange
1 bay leaf	1 bay leaf
salt and pepper	salt and pepper

First make the filling. Fry the minced beef and onion in the oil in a large frying pan until softened and lightly coloured. Stir in the flour then mix in all the remaining filling ingredients. Mix well, bring to the boil and simmer, covered, for 20 minutes. Taste and adjust the seasoning. Cool.

Roll out the pastry and use to line six individual patty cases. Roll out six lids at the same time.

Fill the pastry with the cooled meat mixture, damp the edges of the pastry and cover with the lids. Press the edges together firmly, flute the edges, decorate with leaves from the trimmings and glaze with the beaten egg.

Bake in a moderately hot oven (200°C, 400°F, Gas Mark 6) for 15–20 minutes, or until golden. Remove from the tins and put on serving plates. Carefully raise the lids and put in any extra filling.

Golden Meat Loaf

SERVES 6

METRIC/IMPERIAL	AMERICAN
200 g/8 oz Shortcrust Pastry (see page 132)	½ lb Shortcrust Pastry (see page 132)
beaten egg to glaze	beaten egg to glaze
Meat loaf:	*Meat loaf:*
450 g/1 lb minced steak	1 lb ground steak
225 g/8 oz pork sausagemeat	½ lb pork sausagemeat
1 onion, grated or finely chopped	1 onion, grated or finely chopped
100 g/4 oz fresh breadcrumbs	2 cups fresh soft bread crumbs
1 teaspoon dried thyme	1 teaspoon dried thyme
salt and pepper	salt and pepper
1 egg	1 egg
4 tablespoons fruit chutney	⅓ cup fruit chutney
4 tablespoons tomato ketchup	⅓ cup tomato ketchup

Roll out the pastry to a large oblong about 5 mm/¼ inch thick.

Put all the meat loaf ingredients in a bowl and mix together very well. Press into a loaf shape and put in the centre of the pastry.

Damp the edges of the pastry with cold water and encase the meat, pressing the edges together firmly to seal. Fold the edges under the meat loaf to enclose it completely. Decorate with leaves from the trimmings.

Put on a baking sheet and glaze with the beaten egg. Bake in a moderate oven (180°C, 350°F, Gas Mark 4) for 1½ hours. Serve piping hot, or equally good, serve cold with salad.

Cider Apple Pie

SERVES 8

METRIC/IMPERIAL	AMERICAN
350 g/12 oz Sweet Shortcrust Pastry (see page 132)	¾ lb Sweet Shortcrust Pastry (see page 132)
milk and sugar to glaze	milk and sugar to glaze
100 g/4 oz Cheddar cheese, diced (optional)	1⅓ cups diced Cheddar cheese (optional)
whipped cream for serving	whipped cream for serving
Filling:	*Filling:*
450 ml/¾ pint sweet cider	2 cups sweet cider
900 g/2 lb cooking apples, peeled, cored and sliced	2 lb baking apples, peeled, cored and sliced
100 g/4 oz soft brown sugar	½ cup soft brown sugar
25 g/1 oz plain flour	¼ cup all-purpose flour
1 teaspoon ground mixed spice	1 teaspoon ground mixed spice
1 teaspoon grated lemon rind	1 teaspoon grated lemon rind
50 g/2 oz butter	¼ cup butter

Roll out the pastry and use to line a 20-cm/8-inch shallow cake tin. Roll out the trimmings to a round 23 cm/9 inches across, ready to make a lattice topping.

Put the cider in a saucepan and boil rapidly, uncovered, until reduced to a quarter, about 4 tablespoons (U.S. ⅓ cup). Cool.

Mix together the apples, sugar, flour, spice and lemon rind and spread in the prepared pastry case. Dot with butter.

Cut strips of the pastry 1 cm/½ inch wide and weave strips on top of the pie in a lattice. Damp the pastry so the strips are firmly sealed to the base at each end. Brush with milk and sprinkle with sugar to glaze. Pour the cider into the centre of the pie.

Bake in a moderately hot oven (200°C, 400°F, Gas Mark 6) for 45 minutes or until the apple is cooked and pastry crisp.

If liked, put a cube of cheese in each space of the lattice top. Return to the oven for 3–4 minutes, or until the cheese is just melted. Serve warm, with whipped cream.

Spiced Fruit Pie

SERVES 6

METRIC/IMPERIAL	AMERICAN
175 g/6 oz Shortcrust Pastry (see page 132)	1½ cups Shortcrust Pastry (see page 132)
Filling:	*Filling:*
900 g/2 lb rhubarb, plums, apples or other fruit	2 lb rhubarb, plums, apples or other fruit
2 tablespoons water	3 tablespoons water
100 g/4 oz sugar	½ cup sugar
50 g/2 oz cornflour	½ cup cornstarch
2 tablespoons brandy or orange juice	3 tablespoons brandy or orange juice
Topping:	*Topping:*
40 g/1½ oz plain flour	6 tablespoons all-purpose flour
40 g/1½ oz soft brown sugar	3 tablespoons soft brown sugar
75 g/3 oz butter	6 tablespoons butter
½ teaspoon ground cinnamon	½ teaspoon ground cinnamon
pinch of grated nutmeg	dash of grated nutmeg
whipped cream or ice cream for serving	whipped cream or ice cream for serving

Roll out the pastry and use to line a 20-cm/8-inch shallow cake tin.

Prepare the fruit for stewing according to its type. Put into a saucepan with the water and sugar. Bring to the boil and cook for 3–5 minutes. Mix together the cornflour and brandy or orange juice and stir into the fruit. Cook, stirring all the time, until the liquid is thickened and clear. Cool.

Spread the fruit mixture in the pastry case. To make the topping, rub all the ingredients together until they resemble coarse breadcrumbs. Spread the topping over the fruit.

Bake in a moderately hot oven (200°C, 400°F, Gas Mark 6) for 30–35 minutes or until cooked.

Serve with cream or ice cream.

Holly Berry Mince Pies

MAKES 12 PIES

METRIC/IMPERIAL	AMERICAN
100 g/4 oz Shortcrust Pastry (see page 132)	$\frac{1}{4}$ lb Shortcrust Pastry (see page 132)
5 tablespoons mincemeat	6 tablespoons mincemeat
1 (227-g/8-oz) can red cherries	1 (8-oz) can red cherries
1 teaspoon brandy (optional)	1 teaspoon brandy (optional)
1 egg white	1 egg white
50 g/2 oz castor sugar	$\frac{1}{4}$ cup sugar

Roll out the pastry thinly and use to line 12 patty cases. Prick well with a fork and bake in a moderately hot oven (200°C, 400°F, Gas Mark 6) for 10 minutes, or until just cooked.

Put the mincemeat in a bowl. Drain the cherries, remove the stones and chop the flesh. Reserve some for decoration and stir the rest into the mincemeat with the brandy, if used.

Fill the cooked pastry cases with the mincemeat mixture. Whisk the egg white until stiff and whisk in half the sugar. Whisk until stiff again then fold in the remaining sugar. Pile the meringue on to the pies.

Bake in a moderate oven (160°C, 325°F, Gas Mark 3) for about 20 minutes, or until lightly browned.

Serve hot or cold, decorated with the reserved cherries.

Rum Cakes

MAKES 12 LARGE OR 24 SMALL CAKES.

These are lovely to serve with coffee after dinner.

METRIC/IMPERIAL	AMERICAN
100 g/4 oz Sweet Shortcrust Pastry (see page 132)	$\frac{1}{4}$ lb Sweet Shortcrust Pastry (see page 132)
50 g/2 oz plain chocolate, grated	$\frac{1}{3}$ cup dark chocolate pieces, grated
4 tablespoons double cream, whipped	$\frac{1}{3}$ cup heavy cream, whipped
1 tablespoon rum	1 tablespoon rum
100 g/4 oz icing sugar, sifted	scant 1 cup sifted confectioner's sugar
few drops of green food colouring	few drops of green food coloring

First make the pastry. Roll out thinly on a lightly floured surface, cut out rounds and use to line 12 patty cases or 24 small bouchée cases.

Prick the bases and line each with a small square of foil. Bake in a moderately hot oven (200°C, 400°F, Gas Mark 6) for 15 minutes or until cooked. Cool.

Mix together the chocolate, cream and rum and use to fill the pastry cases.

Mix the icing sugar with a few drops of green food colouring and enough cold water to make a thick but flowing icing. Spoon on to the chocolate mixture to coat.

Serve the same day if possible.

Courgette Lamb Pie

SERVES 4–6

METRIC/IMPERIAL	AMERICAN
1 (368-g/13-oz) packet frozen puff pastry	1 (13-oz) package frozen puff paste
beaten egg to glaze	beaten egg to glaze
Filling:	*Filling:*
675 g/1½ lb lean boneless lamb	1½ lb lean boneless lamb
4 tablespoons oil	⅓ cup oil
2 onions, finely chopped	2 onions, finely chopped
1 clove garlic, crushed	1 clove garlic, crushed
1 tablespoon plain flour	1 tablespoon all-purpose flour
1 (227-g/8-oz) can tomatoes	1 (8-oz) can tomatoes
150 ml/¼ pint stock	⅔ cup stock
salt and pepper	salt and pepper
450 g/1 lb courgettes, sliced	1 lb zucchini, sliced

Thaw the pastry.

Cut the lamb into bite-sized cubes, or ask your butcher to do this for you. Heat half the oil in a large saucepan and fry the onion until softened. Add the lamb and cook, stirring until coloured. Add the garlic and stir in the flour. Add the tomatoes, stock and seasoning. Bring to the boil, stirring all the time. Cover the pan and simmer for 1 hour or until the lamb is tender.

Meanwhile, fry the courgettes in the remaining oil until lightly browned. Drain.

Put the cooked lamb in a pie dish and cover with the courgettes. Roll out the pastry, allowing a lining strip for the rim of the dish. Cover the pie, sealing the edges with beaten egg. Decorate the top with leaves made from the pastry trimmings. Flake and flute the edges and brush with the beaten egg.

Bake in a hot oven (230°C, 450°F, Gas Mark 8) for 20 minutes, or until well risen and golden. Serve as soon as possible.

Steak and Kidney Pie

SERVES 6

METRIC/IMPERIAL	AMERICAN
1 (368-g/13-oz) packet frozen puff pastry	1 (13-oz) package frozen puff paste
beaten egg to glaze	beaten egg to glaze
Filling:	*Filling:*
675 g/1½ lb stewing steak	1½ lb beef stew meat
225 g/8 oz ox kidney	½ lb ox kidney
salt and pepper	salt and pepper
25 g/1 oz plain flour	¼ cup all-purpose flour
2 tablespoons oil	3 tablespoons oil
1 onion, chopped	1 onion, chopped
300 ml/½ pint stock or 150 ml/¼ pint stock and 150 ml/¼ pint red wine	1¼ cups stock or ⅔ cup stock and ⅔ cup red wine
1 bay leaf	1 bay leaf
pinch of dried mixed herbs	dash of dried mixed herbs
100 g/4 oz button mushrooms (optional)	¼ lb mushrooms (optional)

Thaw the pastry.

Cut the steak and kidney into bite-sized pieces, or ask your butcher to do this for you. Season the flour and coat the meat with it. Heat the oil in a large saucepan and fry the onion until softened. Add the meat and any excess flour. Cook, stirring, until coloured. Add the stock (or stock and wine), bay leaf and herbs. Bring to the boil, stirring all the time. Cover and simmer for 1–2 hours, or until the meat is tender (this will depend on the cut of beef you buy).

Add the mushrooms and put the filling in a pie dish. Roll out the pastry, allowing a lining strip for the rim of the dish. Cover the pie, sealing the edges with beaten egg. Decorate the top with leaves made from the pastry trimmings. Flake and flute the edges and brush with the beaten egg.

Bake in a very hot oven (230°C, 450°F, Gas Mark 8) for 20 minutes, or until well risen and golden. Serve as soon as possible.

Chicken Vols-au-vent

SERVES 6

METRIC/IMPERIAL	AMERICAN
6 large frozen vol-au-vent cases	6 large frozen vol-au-vent cases
beaten egg to glaze	beaten egg to glaze
Filling:	*Filling:*
1·5 kg/3 lb roasting chicken	3 lb roasting chicken
1 onion	1 onion
1 lemon, halved	1 lemon, halved
1 bouquet garni	1 bouquet garni
8 peppercorns	8 peppercorns
100 g/4 oz butter	½ cup butter
100 g/4 oz button mushrooms	¼ lb mushrooms
75 g/3 oz plain flour	¾ cup all-purpose flour
150 ml/¼ pint single cream	⅔ cup light cream
salt and pepper	salt and pepper

First prepare the filling. Put the chicken in a saucepan, cover with water and add the onion, lemon, bouquet garni and peppercorns. Bring to the boil, cover the pan and simmer for 1 – 1¼ hours, or until the chicken is cooked.

Remove the chicken from the stock. Strain the stock and reserve 600 ml/1 pint (U.S. 2½ cups). Cool.

Melt the butter in a large saucepan and fry the mushrooms until cooked. Remove and drain on absorbent kitchen paper.

Add the stock and flour to the saucepan and bring to the boil, whisking all the time with a balloon whisk. Whisk until thickened and smooth. Boil for 2 – 3 minutes, stirring continuously.

Remove the chicken from the bones; add it to the sauce with the mushrooms and cream. Reheat without boiling. Taste and adjust the seasoning.

Cook the vol-au-vent cases according to the instructions on the packet. Put the vols-au-vent on serving plates and fill with the chicken sauce so that it spills out amply around the pastry cases. Serve straightaway.

Boxing Day Pie

SERVES 4

METRIC/IMPERIAL	AMERICAN
Hot water crust pastry:	*Hot water crust dough:*
275 g/10 oz plain flour	2½ cups all-purpose flour
½ teaspoon salt	½ teaspoon salt
100 g/4 oz lard	½ cup shortening
6 tablespoons water	½ cup water
beaten egg to glaze	beaten egg to glaze
Filling:	*Filling:*
225 g/8 oz cooked turkey	½ lb cooked turkey
100 g/4 oz ham, diced	½ cup diced cooked ham
1 teaspoon dried mixed herbs	1 teaspoon dried mixed herbs
1 small onion, grated	1 small onion, grated
salt and pepper	salt and pepper
150 ml/¼ pint chicken stock	⅔ cup chicken stock
⅔ (14-g/½-oz) envelope powdered gelatine	1½ (7-g/¼-oz) envelopes gelatin

Line a 0·5-kg/1-lb loaf tin with greaseproof paper to ensure the pie turns out whole.

First make the pastry. Sift the flour and salt into a mixing bowl. Put the lard and water into a saucepan, heat gently until the lard is melted then bring to the boil. Pour the boiling liquid into the flour and mix in quickly with a wooden spoon to make a soft dough. Cool slightly.

Cut off a quarter of the dough and keep warm, covered with a tea towel. Press the remainder into the base-lined tin so that it is evenly lined.

Slice the turkey thinly. Mix the ham with the herbs, onion and seasoning. Layer the turkey and ham in the pastry case. Add 2 tablespoons stock.

Roll out the remaining pastry to make a lid. Brush the edges of the pie with the beaten egg and put the lid on top. Press the edges together firmly to seal. Trim the pastry and decorate the top with leaves made from the pastry trimmings. Place in position, securing them with beaten egg. Crimp the pastry edges and glaze the pie with beaten egg. Make a hole in the centre.

Bake in a moderately hot oven (190°C, 375°F, Gas Mark 5) for 45 minutes. Cool.

Meanwhile, dissolve the gelatine in the remaining stock.

Pour the stock into the pie and leave until completely cold and firm.

Run a knife round the tin, dip the base quickly into very hot water and turn the pie out. Serve cold.

Special Sausage Rolls

MAKES 10 LARGE OR 16 SMALL ROLLS

METRIC/IMPERIAL
1 (212-g/7½-oz) packet frozen puff pastry
225 g/8 oz pork sausagemeat
4 rashers streaky bacon, chopped
pinch of dried sage
salt and pepper
beaten egg to glaze

AMERICAN
1 (7½-oz) package frozen puff paste
½ lb pork sausagemeat
4 bacon slices, chopped
dash of dried sage
salt and pepper
beaten egg to glaze

Thaw the pastry.

Mix together very thoroughly the sausagemeat, bacon, sage and seasoning. Divide the sausagemeat mixture in half. Roll both pieces into a sausage 40 cm/16 inches long.

Roll out the pastry on a lightly floured surface to a rectangle 15 × 40 cm/6 × 16 inches. Cut the pastry in half lengthways.

Place a sausagemeat roll down the centre of each strip. Damp the long edge and either fold the pastry over, or roll the sausagemeat in the pastry. Seal the join firmly. Brush with beaten egg and snip the top with a pair of scissors at 1-cm/½-inch intervals. Cut into 10 or 16 sausage rolls. Put on a baking sheet and bake in a hot oven (220°C, 425°F, Gas Mark 7) for 15 – 25 minutes (according to the size) or until cooked and golden.

Serve hot or warm.

Cream Buns or Éclairs

MAKES ABOUT 10 BUNS

METRIC/IMPERIAL	AMERICAN
Choux pastry:	*Choux paste:*
65 g/2½ oz plain flour	½ cup plus 2 tablespoons all-purpose flour
150 ml/¼ pint water	⅔ cup water
50 g/2 oz butter or margarine	¼ cup butter or margarine
2 eggs, beaten	2 eggs, beaten
Filling:	*Filling:*
150 ml/¼ pint whipping cream	⅔ cup whipping cream
Topping:	*Topping:*
175 g/6 oz icing sugar	1⅓ cups sifted confectioner's sugar
1 tablespoon cocoa powder	1 tablespoon cocoa powder
hot water to mix	hot water to mix

Sift the flour on to a plate and put it in a warm place.

Put the water and butter or margarine into a saucepan and heat gently until the fat is melted. Bring the liquid to the boil then immediately add the flour all at once. Cooking the mixture very gently, mix well with a wooden spoon, beating until the mixture forms a ball and leaves the sides of the pan clean.

Remove the pan from the heat and gradually beat in the eggs. Beat well until smooth and glossy.

Spoon the mixture into a piping bag fitted with a plain nozzle. Pipe the mixture on to a greased baking sheet, making 10 rounds (buns) or 10 long sausage shapes (éclairs), spaced well apart to allow for rising.

Bake in a hot oven (200°C, 400°F, Gas Mark 6) for about 35 minutes or until well risen, golden and dry. Cool on a wire rack.

Whip the cream and use to fill the buns or éclairs.

Sift the icing sugar and cocoa together and stir in enough hot water to make a thick coating icing. Dip the tops of the buns or éclairs into the icing. Put aside until set.

Serve as soon as possible.

Profiteroles

SERVES 6

METRIC/IMPERIAL	AMERICAN
1 quantity Choux Pastry (see left)	1 quantity Choux Paste (see left)
150 ml/¼ pint whipping cream	⅔ cup whipping cream
Chocolate sauce:	*Chocolate sauce:*
300 ml/½ pint milk	1¼ cups milk
50 g/2 oz cocoa powder	½ cup cocoa powder
100 g/4 oz soft brown sugar	½ cup soft brown sugar

Make the pastry, spoon on to a greased baking sheet in small round mounds. Bake in a moderately hot oven (200°C, 400°F, Gas Mark 6) for 20 minutes. Reduce the heat to moderate (180°C, 350°F, Gas Mark 4) and bake for a further 30–40 minutes or until golden, crisp and dry. Cool on a wire rack.

Whip the cream and use to fill the buns.

Put all the sauce ingredients into a saucepan and bring to the boil, stirring well all the time. Boil, stirring, for 2 minutes.

Serve the cream-filled buns with hot chocolate sauce poured over.

Baking

Family baking is something that is done every week. The recipes used are well tried and popular. Occasionally a new recipe is tried out and proves itself a success. In this chapter you will find old and new recipes to try.

When you are baking cakes it is necessary to prepare the cake tin. Whisked sponges and rich fruit cakes need to have the tin lined completely with greased greaseproof paper. It is even a good idea to line the base of tins for not-so-rich cakes, so that you are sure they will turn out without accidents. Follow these simple directions. To line a deep cake tin, cut a double thickness of greaseproof paper, folded along one edge and long enough to go round the tin and overlap a little. It should be 4 cm/1½ inches deeper than the tin. Make a fold 1 cm/½ inch deep along the folded edge of the paper. Snip up to the fold at 1-cm/½-inch intervals. Cut two circles or squares the size of the base of the tin. Grease the tin and the inside of the strip of paper. Put one of the circles or squares on the base of the tin. Put the strip of paper round the sides, fitting the fold snugly into the base with the snipped pieces overlapping on the bottom. Grease the remaining circle or square and fit it on top of the base.

It is especially important in bread making to follow the recipe carefully, as each ingredient has a profound effect on the final product. Use strong bread flour for successful loaves – ordinary flour does not give the bread the same texture. Yeast is nourished by sugar so a little should be added to the mixture, but not too much or the yeast will "over eat" and die. Salt also may seem such a small ingredient but is essential for the flavour of the bread. Too much, however, will kill the yeast. The rising times that doughs need are very variable. The richer the ingredients (eggs, fat and milk), the longer the rising takes, but this is only a small detail, the main factor controlling the rising of dough is the temperature. Yeast works at its best in a warm, moist atmosphere. It will be very retarded if it is put in a cool place and yeast will be killed if it is overheated. So rise your dough in the kitchen, close to the cooker. If you want to delay the rising, it can be done overnight in the refrigerator, but make sure it reaches room temperature again before baking.

Rich Fruit Cake

MAKES ONE (20-cm/8-inch) ROUND CAKE.

Suitable for Christmas, weddings and special occasions – if alcohol is wanted in the cake, when cool, prick it well all over with a skewer and sprinkle with 2 – 3 tablespoons rum, brandy or whisky.

METRIC/IMPERIAL	AMERICAN
225 g/8 oz butter	1 cup butter
225 g/8 oz soft brown sugar	1 cup soft brown sugar
6 eggs	6 eggs
225 g/8 oz plain flour	2 cups all-purpose flour
1½ teaspoons ground mixed spice	1½ teaspoons ground mixed spice
1 tablespoon cocoa powder	1 tablespoon cocoa powder
grated rind and juice of 2 oranges	grated rind and juice of 2 oranges
grated rind and juice of 1 lemon	grated rind and juice of 1 lemon
225 g/8 oz currants	1⅓ cups currants
225 g/8 oz sultanas	1⅓ cups seedless white raisins
225 g/8 oz raisins	1⅓ cups raisins
175 g/6 oz chopped mixed peel	1 cup chopped candied peel
175 g/6 oz glacé cherries, chopped	¾ cup candied cherries, chopped
50 g/2 oz almonds, chopped	½ cup almonds, chopped

Line an 20-cm/8-inch deep round cake tin with greaseproof paper (see page 148) and grease well.

Cream the butter and sugar together until fluffy and light in colour. Beat in the eggs, one at a time. Sift the flour with the spice and cocoa and stir in. Stir in all the remaining ingredients and mix well.

Put the mixture into the prepared tin and spread evenly. Bake in a moderate oven (160°C, 325°F, Gas Mark 3) for 30 minutes. Reduce to cool (150°C, 300°F, Gas Mark 2) for 1 hour. Reduce the oven temperature again, keeping it cool (140°C, 275°F, Gas Mark 1) for a further 2 hours, or until cooked. Test with a skewer – it should come out clean and dry.

Turn the cake out and cool on a wire rack.

Wrap the cake in fresh greaseproof paper and foil and store for at least 1 month before using.

Royal Icing

ENOUGH TO COVER A 20-cm/8-inch ROUND RICH FRUIT CAKE.

This icing can be put directly on to the cake, but the colour tends to come through. A layer of almond paste stops this happening.

METRIC/IMPERIAL	AMERICAN
Almond paste:	*Almond paste:*
225 g/8 oz icing sugar, sifted	1¾ cups sifted confectioner's sugar
225 g/8 oz castor sugar	1 cup sugar
225 g/8 oz ground almonds	2 cups ground almonds
1 egg	1 egg
1 tablespoon lemon juice	1 tablespoon lemon juice
few drops of almond essence	few drops of almond extract
sieved apricot jam	sieved apricot jam
Royal icing:	*Royal icing:*
3 egg whites	3 egg whites
675 g/1½ lb icing sugar, sifted	5¼ cups sifted confectioner's sugar
1 teaspoon glycerine	1 teaspoon glycerine
2 tablespoons lemon juice	3 tablespoons lemon juice

First prepare the almond paste. Mix all the ingredients except the jam together to a firm paste. Roll out on a surface dusted with icing sugar to cover the top and sides of the cake. Do this by rolling a circle and a strip to fit the cake. Warm the jam slightly and brush the top and sides of the cake before covering with the almond paste. Leave to dry for 1 – 2 days if possible, before covering with the icing.

Put the egg whites in a large bowl. Gradually add the sifted icing sugar beating well with a wooden spoon all the time.

Add the glycerine and lemon juice and beat until the icing is glossy and will stand in soft peaks. Cover with cling film or a damp tea towel if you are not going to use the icing straightaway.

If the icing is too firm, add a little more lemon juice. If it is not stiff enough (perhaps you need the icing for piping) beat in a little more icing sugar.

Spread the icing over the cake, roughing the surface or smoothing as required. Leave for at least 1 – 2 days to set before serving.

One-stage Victoria Sandwich

MAKES ONE 18-cm/7-inch CAKE

METRIC/IMPERIAL	AMERICAN
175 g/6 oz soft margarine	¾ cup soft margarine
175 g/6 oz castor sugar	¾ cup sugar
3 eggs	3 eggs
175 g/6 oz self-raising flour	1½ cups all-purpose flour sifted with 3 teaspoons baking powder
1½ teaspoons baking powder	
1 quantity Butter Icing (see opposite) or 3 tablespoons jam	1 quantity Butter Icing (see opposite) or ¼ cup jam
icing sugar to dust	confectioner's sugar to dust

Line two 15-cm/7-inch sandwich tins with a circle of greaseproof paper and grease the base and sides well.

Put the margarine, sugar and eggs into a mixing bowl. Sift in the flour and baking powder together. Beat for 2–3 minutes, until well mixed.

Divide the cake mixture between the tins and spread evenly. Bake in a moderate oven (160°C, 325°F, Gas Mark 3) for 30–35 minutes or until well risen, golden and firm to touch. Remove the cakes from the tins and cool on a wire rack.

Sandwich together with Butter Icing (see opposite) or jam and dust the top with sifted icing sugar.

Variations

Chocolate sandwich Replace 3 tablespoons (U.S. ¼ cup) of the flour with cocoa. Sandwich with Chocolate or Peppermint Butter Icing (see opposite).

Orange or lemon sandwich Add the finely grated rind of 1 small orange or lemon with 1 tablespoon of the juice. Sandwich with the appropriate flavour of Butter Icing (see opposite) or with marmalade.

Coffee sandwich Dissolve 2 teaspoons of coffee essence in 1 tablespoon boiling water. Cool and add to the mixture. Sandwich with Coffee Butter Icing (see opposite).

Butter Icing

ENOUGH TO FILL ONE 18-cm/7-inch SANDWICH CAKE.

Make twice this quantity if you want to ice the top of the cake as well.

METRIC/IMPERIAL	AMERICAN
50 g/2 oz butter, softened	¼ cup butter, softened
100 g/4 oz icing sugar, sifted	scant 1 cup sifted confectioner's sugar
1 tablespoon hot water	1 tablespoon hot water
few drops of vanilla essence	few drops of vanilla extract

Beat the butter then gradually beat in the icing sugar. Add the hot water and vanilla essence to make a smooth icing. Use as required.

Variations

Chocolate butter icing Dissolve 1 tablespoon cocoa powder in the hot water.

Coffee butter icing Dissolve 2 teaspoons instant coffee in the hot water.

Orange or lemon butter icing Add the finely grated rind of ½ orange or lemon. Use juice from the fruit instead of hot water.

Peppermint butter icing Use peppermint essence instead of vanilla.

Strawberry and Cream Cake

MAKES ONE 18-cm/7-inch SANDWICH CAKE.

Other fruit, fresh, canned or frozen can of course be used for this cake.

METRIC/IMPERIAL	AMERICAN
Whisked sponge:	*Whisked cake batter:*
3 eggs	3 eggs
100 g/4 oz castor sugar	$\frac{1}{2}$ cup sugar
100 g/4 oz self-raising flour	1 cup all-purpose flour sifted with 1 teaspoon baking powder
50 g/2 oz butter, melted	$\frac{1}{4}$ cup butter, melted
icing sugar to dust	confectioner's sugar to dust
Filling:	*Filling:*
150 ml/$\frac{1}{4}$ pint whipping cream	$\frac{2}{3}$ cup whipping cream
225 g/8 oz strawberries	$\frac{1}{2}$ lb strawberries

Line two 18-cm/7-inch shallow cake tins with circles of greaseproof paper. Grease the base and sides well.

Put the eggs and sugar in a mixing bowl and whisk well until the mixture is soft and light. It should be thick enough for a whisk to leave a trail. (If you have not got an electric mixer this will have to be done in a basin over a saucepan of simmering water). Sift the flour and fold in very gently, alternating with the butter.

Divide the cake mixture between the tins and spread evenly. Bake in a moderate oven (180°C, 350°F, Gas Mark 4) for 20–25 minutes, or until well risen, golden and firm.

Turn the cakes out of the tins and cool on a wire rack.

Whip the cream. Halve the strawberries. Spread half the cream over one cake, top with the strawberries and sift some icing sugar on top. Cover with the remaining cake. Pipe the remaining cream on top and dust the top with sifted icing sugar. Serve as soon as possible. Store any leftover cake in an airtight container in the refrigerator.

Tia Maria Gâteau

SERVES 8

A very special gâteau which makes a lovely dessert.

METRIC/IMPERIAL

1 quantity whisked sponge
  (see Strawberry and
  Cream Cake)
Filling:
50 g/2 oz butter
75 g/3 oz icing sugar, sifted
50 g/2 oz ground almonds
25 g/1 oz cocoa powder
1 egg yolk
2 tablespoons strong black
  coffee
1 tablespoon Tia Maria
For soaking:
150 ml/¼ pint strong black
  coffee
4 tablespoons Tia Maria
For decoration:
300 ml/½ pint whipping
  cream
50 g/2 oz flaked almonds

AMERICAN

1 quantity whisked cake
  batter (see Strawberry
  and Cream Cake)
Filling:
¼ cup butter
⅔ cup sifted confectioner's
  sugar
½ cup ground almonds
¼ cup cocoa powder
1 egg yolk
3 tablespoons
  strong black coffee
1 tablespoon Tia Maria
For soaking:
⅔ cup strong black coffee
⅓ cup Tia Maria
For decoration:
1¼ cups whipping cream
½ cup flaked almonds

First prepare the sponge. Put it in a greased and lined 18-cm/7-inch deep cake tin and bake in a moderate oven (180°C, 350°F, Gas Mark 4) for 30–40 minutes, or until well risen, golden and firm. Turn out of the tin and cool on a wire rack.

Make the filling by beating all the filling ingredients together. Slice the cake into three layers. Put a circle of greaseproof paper in the base of the tin in which the cake was baked and grease well.

Mix together the coffee and Tia Maria for soaking. Put a layer of cake in the tin, sprinkle with one-third of the soaking mixture. Spread over half the filling. Top with another layer of cake and sprinkle again with half of the remaining mixture. Spread the remaining filling on top then cover with the last layer of cake. Sprinkle with the remaining soaking mixture.

Cover the cake with greaseproof paper and press with a small plate with a weight on top. Leave for at least 4 hours.

Turn the cake out of the tin. Whip the cream, use to cover the cake and pipe rosettes on top. Toast the almonds under a grill until lightly browned. Cool then press the nuts over the sides of the cake and sprinkle a few on top.

Chill well before serving. Store any leftover gâteau in an airtight container in the refrigerator.

Meringues

MAKES 8 – 10 CREAM-FILLED MERINGUES

METRIC/IMPERIAL	AMERICAN
2 egg whites	2 egg whites
100 g/4 oz castor sugar	$\frac{1}{2}$ cup sugar
150 ml/$\frac{1}{4}$ pint double cream	$\frac{1}{3}$ cup heavy cream

Line a baking sheet with greaseproof paper and grease lightly.

Put the egg whites in a clean, dry mixing bowl and whisk very well until they are snowy and stand in soft peaks. Sprinkle half the sugar into the bowl and whisk until stiff again. Fold the remaining sugar into the mixture very gently using a metal tablespoon.

Pipe or spoon 16 or 20 meringues on to the prepared baking sheet.

Leave to dry out in the oven at the lowest possible temperature, until they are thoroughly dry and not sticky at all. This will take about 8 hours.

Cool the meringues on a wire rack. Whip the cream until stiff and sandwich the meringues together in pairs. Serve as soon as possible.

The unfilled meringues can be stored in an airtight tin for 3 – 4 weeks until required.

Malt Loaf

MAKES 1 LOAF.

Buy malt extract from the chemist or health food shop.

METRIC/IMPERIAL	AMERICAN
350 g/12 oz plain flour	3 cups all-purpose flour
1 teaspoon baking powder	1 teaspoon baking powder
$\frac{1}{2}$ teaspoon bicarbonate of soda	$\frac{1}{2}$ teaspoon baking soda
50 g/2 oz soft brown sugar	$\frac{1}{4}$ cup soft brown sugar
225 g/8 oz sultanas	$1\frac{1}{3}$ cups seedless white raisins
4 tablespoons malt extract	$\frac{1}{2}$ cup malt extract
4 tablespoons golden syrup	$\frac{1}{3}$ cup corn syrup
4 tablespoons milk	$\frac{1}{3}$ cup milk
2 eggs	2 eggs

Sift the flour, baking powder and bicarbonate of soda into a bowl. Stir in the sugar and sultanas. Put the malt extract, syrup and milk into a saucepan and heat gently, stirring, until mixed and smooth. Mix the warm malt mixture into the flour and stir well until well mixed. Beat in the eggs.

Line a 1-kg/2-lb loaf tin with greased greaseproof paper. Put in the cake mixture and spread it evenly. Bake in a moderate oven (160°C, 325°F, Gas Mark 3) for $1\frac{1}{2}$ hours, or until cooked.

Turn the loaf out of the tin and cool on a wire rack. Serve sliced and buttered.

Apricot Bran Teabread

MAKES ONE 15-cm/6-inch ROUND CAKE

Buy bran from a health food shop. Serve this teabread with butter.

METRIC/IMPERIAL	AMERICAN
225 g/8 oz self-raising flour	2 cups all-purpose flour sifted with 2 teaspoons baking powder
pinch of salt	dash of salt
175 g/6 oz soft brown sugar	¾ cup soft brown sugar
175 g/6 oz dried apricots, chopped	1 cup dried apricots, chopped
300 ml/½ pint milk	1¼ cups milk
2 tablespoons treacle	3 tablespoons molasses
100 g/4 oz bran	2 cups bran
1 egg	1 egg
50 g/2 oz butter, melted	¼ cup butter, melted

Grease a deep 15-cm/6-inch cake tin.

Sift the flour and salt into a mixing bowl. Stir in the sugar and apricots until well mixed.

Mix all the remaining ingredients together then stir them into the apricot mixture.

Spread the mixture evenly in the tin. Bake in a moderate oven (180°C, 350°F, Gas Mark 4) for about 1¾ hours, or until well risen, golden and firm. Turn the cake out of the tin and cool on a wire rack.

Chocolate Fudge Cake

MAKES ONE 20-cm/8-inch CAKE

A special occasion cake.

METRIC/IMPERIAL	AMERICAN
175 g/6 oz plain chocolate	1 cup dark chocolate pieces
175 g/6 oz butter	¾ cup butter
350 g/12 oz soft brown sugar	1½ cups soft brown sugar
4 large eggs	4 large eggs
1 teaspoon vanilla essence	1 teaspoon vanilla extract
225 g/8 oz self-raising flour	2 cups all-purpose flour sifted with 2 teaspoons baking powder
300 ml/½ pint milk	1¼ cups milk
Soured cream icing:	*Sour cream frosting:*
450 g/1 lb plain chocolate	1⅔ cups dark chocolate pieces
2 (142-ml/5-fl oz) cartons soured cream	2 (5-fl oz) cartons dairy sour cream

Base line three 20-cm/8-inch shallow cake tins with greaseproof paper and grease the sides well.

Break the chocolate into pieces and put into a basin. Put over a saucepan of simmering water until the chocolate has melted.

Cream the butter and sugar together until light and fluffy. Beat in the eggs, one at a time, then work in the melted chocolate and vanilla essence. Sift the flour and fold into the mixture very gently, alternating with the milk.

Divide the mixture between the three tins and spread evenly. Bake in a moderately hot oven (190°C, 375°F, Gas Mark 5) for 25–30 minutes or until firm and cooked. Remove the cakes from the tins and cool.

To make the soured cream icing, melt the chocolate in a basin over simmering water, as before. Stir in the cream and use while still warm.

Sandwich the completely cold cakes together with 5 mm/¼ inch icing. Spread the remaining icing quickly over the top and sides of the cake.

Serve as soon as possible. Any leftover cake should be stored in an airtight container in the refrigerator.

Note: If you have not got three 20-cm/8-inch sandwich tins, use one deep 20-cm/8-inch cake tin. Cook in a moderate oven (180°C, 350°F, Gas Mark 4) for about 1¼ hours.

Orange and Lemon Gingerbread

Christmas Shortcake

MAKES ONE 18-cm/7-inch SQUARE GINGERBREAD

METRIC/IMPERIAL	AMERICAN
225 g/8 oz plain flour	2 cups all-purpose flour
2 teaspoons ground ginger	2 teaspoons ground ginger
½ teaspoon bicarbonate of soda	½ teaspoon baking soda
pinch of salt	dash of salt
finely grated rind and juice of 1 orange	finely grated rind and juice of 1 orange
finely grated rind and juice of 1 lemon	finely grated rind and juice of 1 lemon
100 g/4 oz soft brown sugar	½ cup soft brown sugar
75 g/3 oz butter	6 tablespoons butter
175 g/6 oz golden syrup	½ cup corn syrup
1 egg, beaten	1 egg, beaten
225 g/8 oz icing sugar, sifted	1¾ cups sifted confectioner's sugar
crystallised ginger	candied ginger

Line a 20-cm/8-inch deep cake tin with greaseproof paper and grease well.

Sift the flour, ginger, bicarbonate of soda and salt into a mixing bowl. Add the orange and lemon rind. Put the sugar, butter and syrup into a saucepan. Stir over a low heat until melted and combined. Stir in the orange juice then the egg. Pour the melted mixture into the flour and stir to mix well.

Pour into the prepared tin and spread evenly. Bake in a moderate oven (180°C, 350°F, Gas Mark 4) for 45 minutes–1 hour, or until well risen and firm.

Turn the cake out and cool on a wire rack.

Sift the icing sugar and mix with about 2 tablespoons (U.S. 3 tablespoons) of the lemon juice to make a coating icing. Chop the crystallised ginger. Ice the gingerbread and scatter with the ginger pieces.

MAKES ONE 20-cm/8-inch CAKE

METRIC/IMPERIAL	AMERICAN
100 g/4 oz butter	½ cup butter
175 g/6 oz castor sugar	¾ cup sugar
1 egg	1 egg
225 g/8 oz self-raising flour	2 cups all-purpose flour sifted with 2 teaspoons baking powder
3 tablespoons mincemeat	¼ cup mincemeat
50 g/2 oz flaked almonds	½ cup flaked almonds
icing sugar to dust (optional)	confectioner's sugar to dust (optional)

Line a 20-cm/8-inch shallow cake tin with a circle of greaseproof paper and grease the base and sides well.

Cream the butter and sugar together until light then beat in the egg. Sift the flour and add gradually to make a soft dough.

Divide the dough in half and press one half over the base of the prepared tin. Spread the mincemeat over the dough. Roll the remaining dough, between two pieces of greaseproof paper, to a 20-cm/8-inch round. Place it over the mincemeat and press down gently. Scatter the almonds over the top.

Bake in a moderately hot oven (190°C, 375°F, Gas Mark 5) for 40–50 minutes, or until firm and golden.

Remove the shortcake from the tin and cool on a wire rack. Serve dusted with sifted icing sugar.

Peppermint Slice

MAKES 12 SLICES

METRIC/IMPERIAL	AMERICAN
Biscuit:	*Cookie:*
175 g/6 oz butter	$\frac{3}{4}$ cup butter
225 g/8 oz castor sugar	1 cup sugar
2 eggs	2 eggs
few drops of peppermint essence	few drops of peppermint extract
50 g/2 oz plain flour	$\frac{1}{2}$ cup all-purpose flour
25 g/1 oz cocoa powder	$\frac{1}{4}$ cup cocoa powder
50 g/2 oz ground almonds	$\frac{1}{2}$ cup ground almonds
Cream topping:	*Cream topping:*
50 g/2 oz butter	$\frac{1}{4}$ cup butter
150 g/5 oz icing sugar, sifted	$1\frac{1}{4}$ cups sifted confectioner's sugar
1 tablespoon milk	1 tablespoon milk
1 teaspoon peppermint essence	1 teaspoon peppermint extract
few drops of green food colouring	few drops of green food coloring
175 g/6 oz plain chocolate	1 cup dark chocolate pieces

First make the biscuit. Cream the butter and sugar together then beat in the eggs, one at a time. Stir in the peppermint essence. Sift the flour and cocoa and stir in, with the ground almonds. Spread the mixture in a 20 × 30-cm/8 × 12-inch Swiss roll tin. Bake in a moderate oven (180°C, 350°F, Gas Mark 4) for about 35 minutes. Allow to cool in the tin.

To make the cream topping, beat all the ingredients together, except the chocolate. Spread the mixture over the cooled cooked base and chill until set.

Melt the chocolate in a basin over a saucepan of hot water. Spread over the peppermint topping then chill until set.

To serve, cut into slices with a sharp knife dipped in very hot water.

Yum-yum Biscuits

MAKES 20—30 BISCUITS

So-called by my children!

METRIC/IMPERIAL	AMERICAN
75 g/3 oz plain chocolate	$\frac{1}{2}$ cup dark chocolate pieces
100 g/4 oz butter	$\frac{1}{2}$ cup butter
175 g/6 oz soft brown sugar	$\frac{3}{4}$ cup soft brown sugar
1 egg	1 egg
few drops of coffee essence	few drops of coffee extract
100 g/4 oz cream cheese	$\frac{1}{4}$ lb cream cheese
225 g/8 oz self-raising flour	2 cups all-purpose flour sifted with 2 teaspoons baking powder
25 g/1 oz desiccated coconut	$\frac{1}{3}$ cup shredded coconut
Icing:	*Frosting:*
150 g/5 oz icing sugar, sifted	$1\frac{1}{4}$ cups sifted confectioner's sugar
25 g/1 oz plain chocolate	1 square dark chocolate
$\frac{1}{2}$ tablespoon butter	$\frac{1}{2}$ tablespoon butter
1 tablespoon water	1 tablespoon water
chocolate buttons for decoration	chocolate buttons for decoration

Melt the chocolate in a basin over a saucepan of simmering water. Cream the butter and sugar together until light and fluffy. Beat in the egg then the coffee essence and cream cheese and melted chocolate. Sift the flour and stir in with the coconut.

Drop the mixture in large teaspoonfuls on a greased baking sheet.

Bake in a moderate oven (180°C, 350°F, Gas Mark 4) for 20—25 minutes, or until cooked. Remove from the baking sheet and cool on a wire rack.

To make the chocolate icing, put all the ingredients except the buttons in a basin and stand it over a saucepan of simmering water. Stir until smooth and shiny.

Ice the tops of the biscuits and top each with a chocolate button.

Shortbread

MAKES 8 BISCUITS

METRIC/IMPERIAL	AMERICAN
100 g/4 oz butter	$\frac{1}{2}$ cup butter
50 g/2 oz castor sugar	$\frac{1}{4}$ cup sugar
150 g/5 oz plain flour	$1\frac{1}{4}$ cups all-purpose flour
25 g/1 oz semolina or rice flour	3 tablespoons semolina or rice flour
castor sugar to sprinkle	sugar to sprinkle

Grease an 18-cm/7-inch shallow cake tin.

Cream the butter and sugar together until light and fluffy. Sift in the flour with the semolina or rice flour. Stir in, mixing with your hand, and knead to a smooth dough.

Press the dough into the cake tin. Prick the top with a fork, flute the edges using a thumb and finger and mark into eight wedges with a knife.

Bake in a moderate oven (160°C, 325°F, Gas Mark 3) for 35–40 minutes.

Cool the shortbread in the tin, then, when quite cold, remove from the tin and sprinkle the top with sugar.

Scones

MAKES 10 – 12 SCONES

These can also be made into a scone round – bake this for 5 – 10 minutes longer.

METRIC/IMPERIAL	AMERICAN
225 g/8 oz self-raising flour	2 cups all-purpose flour sifted with 2 teaspoons baking powder
½ teaspoon salt	½ teaspoon salt
50 g/2 oz butter	¼ cup butter
about 150 ml/¼ pint milk	about ⅔ cup milk

Sift the flour and salt into a mixing bowl. Add the butter and rub in using your fingertips until the mixture resembles breadcrumbs. Stir in enough milk to make a soft dough.

Knead lightly on a floured surface then roll out to 1 cm/½ inch thick. Cut out scones using a 5-cm/2-inch cutter, dipped in flour to prevent sticking.

Put the scones on a baking sheet and bake in a hot oven (220°C, 425°F, Gas Mark 7) for 15 minutes or until well risen, golden and cooked.

Serve warm or cold. They are best eaten as soon as possible.

Variations

Cheese scones Sift 1 teaspoon dry mustard with the flour. Stir 50 g/2 oz (U.S. ½ cup) grated dry Cheddar cheese into the rubbed-in mixture.

Fruit scones Stir 25 g/1 oz (U.S. 2 tablespoons) castor sugar and 50 g/2 oz (U.S. ⅓ cup) dried fruit into the rubbed in mixture.

Wholewheat scones Replace 100 g/4 oz (U.S. 1 cup) of the flour with 100 g/4 oz (U.S. 1 cup) wholewheat self-raising flour.

Apple Scone Round

MAKES 8 SCONE WEDGES

Serve well buttered.

METRIC/IMPERIAL
225 g/8 oz self-raising flour
pinch of ground cinnamon
½ teaspoon salt
50 g/2 oz butter
25 g/1 oz castor sugar
1 dessert apple, peeled and cored
6 – 8 tablespoons milk
demerara sugar to sprinkle

AMERICAN
2 cups all-purpose flour sifted with 2 teaspoons baking powder
dash of ground cinnamon
½ teaspoon salt
¼ cup butter
2 tablespoons sugar
1 dessert apple, peeled and cored
about ½ cup milk
light brown sugar to sprinkle

Sift the flour, cinnamon and salt into a mixing bowl. Add the butter and rub in using your fingertips until the mixture resembles breadcrumbs. Stir in the sugar. Grate the apple into the scone mixture. Mix gently with a fork and add enough milk to make a soft dough.

Knead lightly on a floured surface and shape into a round about 2·5 – 4 cm/1 – 1½ inches thick. Place it on a baking sheet. Brush with milk and sprinkle with demerara sugar. Mark the top into eight wedges.

Bake in a hot oven (220°C, 425°F, Gas Mark 7) for 35 minutes, or until cooked. Serve warm if possible.

Hot Cross Buns

MAKES 12 BUNS

METRIC/IMPERIAL	AMERICAN
1 tablespoon dried yeast	1½ packages active dry yeast
4 tablespoons lukewarm water	⅓ cup lukewarm water
50 g/2 oz castor sugar	¼ cup sugar
450 g/1 lb strong bread flour	4 cups all-purpose flour
150 ml/¼ pint milk, warmed	⅔ cups milk, warmed
1 teaspoon salt	1 teaspoon salt
1 teaspoon ground mixed spice	1 teaspoon ground mixed spice
½ teaspoon ground cinnamon	½ teaspoon ground cinnamon
50 g/2 oz butter	¼ cup butter
100 g/4 oz sultanas	⅔ cup seedless white raisins
50 g/2 oz chopped mixed peel	⅓ cup chopped candied peel
1 egg, beaten	1 egg, beaten
Glaze:	Glaze:
50 g/2 oz granulated sugar	¼ cup sugar
3 tablespoons milk	¼ cup milk
Icing:	Frosting:
100 g/4 oz icing sugar	scant 1 cup sifted confectioner's sugar
lemon juice to mix	lemon juice to mix

Stir the yeast into the water with 1 teaspoon of the castor sugar. Put aside in a warm place until frothy, about 10 minutes.

Put 100 g/4 oz (U.S. 1 cup) of the flour in a bowl. Beat in the yeast mixture and milk until smooth. Leave in a warm place until frothy, about 20 minutes.

Sift the remaining flour into a bowl with the salt, spice and cinnamon. Rub in the butter using your fingertips. Stir in the yeast mixture, remaining sugar, sultanas, peel and egg to make a soft dough.

Knead well on a floured surface until smooth and elastic, about 5 minutes.

Put the dough in a lightly oiled polythene bag and leave in a warm place until doubled in bulk, about 1 – 1½ hours.

Knead the dough for a further 2 – 3 minutes and shape into 12 buns. Put the buns on a greased baking sheet. Cover with oiled polythene and leave in a warm place until doubled in size, about 45 minutes – 1 hour. Mark a cross on top of each bun with a sharp knife.

Bake in a hot oven (220°C, 425°F, Gas Mark 7) for 20 – 25 minutes or until well risen, golden and cooked.

To make the glaze, dissolve the sugar in the milk, heating gently without boiling.

Brush the glaze over the buns as soon as they come out of the oven.

For the icing, mix the icing sugar with enough lemon juice to a stiff consistency. Pipe a cross in the marks on top of the buns when cold. Serve the same day if possible.

Soft Bran Rolls

MAKES 12 ROLLS

METRIC/IMPERIAL	AMERICAN
2 teaspoons dried yeast	1 package active dry yeast
150 ml/¼ pint lukewarm water	⅔ cup lukewarm water
75 g/3 oz castor sugar	6 tablespoons sugar
100 g/4 oz margarine	½ cup margarine
3 – 4 tablespoons boiling water	4 – 5 tablespoons boiling water
25 g/1 oz bran	½ cup bran
400 g/14 oz strong bread flour	3½ cups all-purpose flour
1 teaspoon salt	1 teaspoon salt
1 egg	1 egg

Stir the yeast into the water with 1 teaspoon of the sugar. Put in a warm place until frothy on top, about 10 minutes.

Melt the margarine in the boiling water. Put the bran, flour and salt into a mixing bowl and stir in the margarine and water. Cool to lukewarm then stir in the yeast mixture and egg.

Knead the dough on a floured surface for 5 minutes, or until smooth and elastic. Put in a lightly oiled polythene bag and leave in a warm place until doubled in bulk, about 1½ hours.

Knead the dough for a further 2 – 3 minutes then shape into 12 rolls. Put on a greased baking sheet, cover with the oiled polythene bag and leave until doubled in size again, about 1 hour.

Bake in a hot oven (220°C, 425°F, Gas Mark 7) for 15 – 20 minutes, or until cooked.

Wholemeal Apple Sultana Loaf

MAKES 1 COTTAGE LOAF

METRIC / IMPERIAL	AMERICAN
2 teaspoons dried yeast	1 package active dry yeast
150 ml/¼ pint lukewarm water	⅔ cup lukewarm water
2 tablespoons honey	3 tablespoons honey
50 g/2 oz margarine, softened	¼ cup margarine, softened
1 small apple, peeled, cored and grated	1 small apple, peeled, cored and grated
75 g/3 oz sultanas	½ cup seedless white raisins
350 g/12 oz plain wholemeal flour	3 cups wholemeal flour

Stir the yeast into the water with 1 teaspoon of the honey. Put aside in a warm place until frothy on top, about 10 minutes.

Put all the remaining ingredients into a mixing bowl. Add the yeast liquid and mix thoroughly until well combined.

Knead for 5 minutes on a floured surface until smooth and elastic. Put the dough in a lightly oiled polythene bag and leave in a warm place until doubled in bulk, about 1½ hours.

Knead the dough for a further 2 – 3 minutes. Cut off about one-fifth of the dough. Shape the larger piece into a smooth round loaf and place on a greased baking sheet. Shape the remaining portion into a small round and place on top. Press the lightly floured handle of a wooden spoon down through the small loaf into the large loaf to secure them together and remove the spoon handle gently.

Bake in a moderately hot oven (190°C, 375°F, Gas Mark 5) for 45 minutes. Remove the loaf from the baking sheet and cool on a wire rack. Serve as soon as possible.

If there is some left over, store in an airtight container in the refrigerator.

Pizza

SERVES 4 – 6

METRIC/IMPERIAL

Base:
1 teaspoon dried yeast
150 ml/¼ pint lukewarm
  milk and water, mixed
½ teaspoon castor sugar
225 g/8 oz strong bread
  flour
½ teaspoon salt
1 tablespoon olive oil
Topping:
2 tablespoons olive oil
1 large onion, chopped
1 clove garlic, crushed
450 g/1 lb tomatoes, peeled
  and chopped
½ teaspoon dried basil
salt and pepper
175 g/6 oz Mozzarella
  cheese
1 (56-g/2-oz) can anchovy
  fillets
12 black olives, stoned
olive oil to brush

AMERICAN

Base:
½ package active dry yeast
½ cup lukewarm milk and
  water mixed
½ teaspoon sugar
2 cups all-purpose flour
½ teaspoon salt
1 tablespoon olive oil
Topping:
3 tablespoons olive oil
1 large onion, chopped
1 clove garlic, crushed
1 lb tomatoes, peeled and
  chopped
½ teaspoon dried basil
salt and pepper
6 oz Mozzarella cheese
1 (2-oz) can anchovy fillets
12 ripe olives, pitted
olive oil to brush

First make the base. Stir the yeast into the milk and water with the sugar. Leave in a warm place until frothy, about 10 minutes.

Sift the flour and salt into a mixing bowl. Stir in the yeast liquid and oil and mix to make a soft dough. Knead on a floured surface until smooth and elastic, about 5 minutes. Put the dough in a lightly oiled polythene bag and leave in a warm place until doubled in bulk, about 1 hour.

Heat the oil and fry the onion and garlic until softened. Add the tomatoes, basil and seasoning. Cook, stirring, until soft and pulpy.

Roll out the dough to a 23-cm/9-inch round and place it on a greased baking sheet.

Spread the tomato mixture over the dough and arrange thin slices of Mozzarella on top. Cover with a lattice of anchovy fillets and place the olives in the spaces inbetween. Leave in a warm place for 20 minutes. Brush with oil and bake in a hot oven (220°C, 425°F, Gas Mark 7) for about 30 minutes, or until cooked.

Speedy Wholemeal Bread

MAKES 1 SMALL LOAF AND 6 ROLLS

METRIC / IMPERIAL

2 teaspoons dried yeast
300 ml/½ pint lukewarm
  water
2 teaspoons castor sugar
225 g/8 oz strong bread
  flour
225 g/8 oz wholemeal flour
2 teaspoons salt
15 g/½ oz lard

AMERICAN

1 package active dry yeast
1¼ cups lukewarm water
2 teaspoons sugar
2 cups all-purpose flour
2 cups whole meal flour
2 teaspoons salt
1 tablespoon shortening

Stir the yeast into the water with 1 teaspoon of the sugar. Put aside in a warm place until frothy on top, about 10 minutes.

Put the flours into a bowl with the remaining sugar and the salt. Mix well then rub in the lard using your fingertips.

Add the frothy yeast liquid and mix to a soft dough.

Knead the dough on a floured surface for about 5 minutes or until smooth and elastic. Shape the dough into six small rolls and one loaf. Put the rolls on a greased baking sheet and the loaf in a greased 0·5-kg/1-lb loaf tin. Cover with a piece of lightly oiled polythene and leave in a warm place until doubled in bulk, about 1 hour.

Bake in a hot oven (230°C, 450°F, Gas Mark 8) for 15 – 20 minutes for the rolls, 30 – 35 minutes for the loaf, or until well risen, golden and cooked.

Remove from the baking sheet or tin and cool on a wire rack.

Bacon and Cheese Cob

MAKES 1 ROUND LOAF

METRIC/IMPERIAL
225 g/8 oz streaky bacon, chopped
6 tablespoons oil
2 teaspoons dried yeast
150 ml/¼ pint lukewarm water
1 teaspoon castor sugar
1 teaspoon salt
450 g/1 lb strong bread flour
3 eggs
100 g/4 oz Cheddar cheese, grated

AMERICAN
½ lb bacon slices, chopped
½ cup oil
1 package active dry yeast
⅔ cup lukewarm water
1 teaspoon sugar
1 teaspoon salt
4 cups all-purpose flour
3 eggs
1 cup grated Cheddar cheese

Fry the bacon in its own fat until crisp. Drain and add the fat to the oil. Reserve the bacon.

Stir the yeast into the water with the sugar. Put aside in a warm place until frothy on top, about 10 minutes.

Sift the salt and flour together into a mixing bowl. Add the eggs, oil and bacon fat and yeast liquid. Mix to make a soft dough.

Knead well on a floured surface for about 5 minutes, until smooth and elastic.

Put the dough in a lightly oiled polythene bag and leave in a warm place until doubled in bulk, about 4 hours.

Knead the dough for a further 2 – 3 minutes. Fold the bacon and cheese into the dough and knead until incorporated. Shape into a large smooth ball and place in a greased 23-cm/9-inch shallow cake tin. Cover with the oiled polythene bag and leave until doubled in bulk again.

Bake in a moderately hot oven (190°C, 375°F, Gas Mark 5) for about 1 hour or until well risen, golden and cooked.

Remove the loaf from the tin and cool on a wire rack. Serve warm, in buttered slices.

Index